RON WHITE

WRITING

ADVANCED

OXFORD SUPPLEMENTARY SKILLS

SERIES EDITOR: ALAN MALEY

OXFORD UNIVERSITY PRESS

Oxford University Press
Walton Street, Oxford OX2 6DP

Oxford New York Toronto
Delhi Bombay Calcutta Madras Karachi
Petaling Jaya Singapore Hong Kong Tokyo
Nairobi Dar es Salaam Cape Town
Melbourne Auckland

and associated companies in
Beirut Berlin Ibadan Nicosia

Oxford and *Oxford English* are trade marks of
Oxford University Press

ISBN 0 19 453407 3

Set by Promenade Graphics Ltd, Cheltenham

Printed in Hong Kong

Illustrations by:

Bill Belcher
Lorna Turpin

The publishers would like to thank the following for
their permission to reproduce photographs:

Ashmolean Museum, Oxford
Robert Harding Picture Library
Rex Features

The author and publishers would like to thank all the
copyright holders for their permission to reproduce the
extracts in this book.

'A life in the day of Kathy Coulter', *The Sunday Times
Magazine*; Jean Aitchison, *Language Change: Progress or
Decay?*, Fontana; Robert Ardrey, *The Social Contract*,
Fontana; Claire Bretecher, *More Frustration*, Methuen;
Jerome S. Bruner, 'On Coping and Defending', *Toward a
Theory of Instruction*; W. W. Norton; Anthony Burgess,
Earthly Powers; Hutchison; Geoffrey Canon, 'The Food
Scandal', *The Times*; Consumers' Association, *Which?
Way to Run your Car*, Hodder and Stoughton; Peter
Fleming, *News from Tartary*, Macdonald Futura; Giles
Gordon, 'Slovenly Queues' *The Sunday Times*; Somerset
W. Maugham, 'The Luncheon', *Collected Short Stories of
W. Somerset Maugham*; Mary McCarthy *The Stones of
Florence*, Heinemann; Alan Moorehead, *The Fatal
Impact*, Hamish Hamilton; George Orwell, 'England Your
England' and 'Shooting an Elephant', *Inside the Whale and
Other Essays*; Jonathan Raban, *Old Glory*, Flamingo;
Claudia Roden, *Coffee*, Penguin Books; *Roget's
Thesaurus*, Longman; Jean Sargeant 'Moving Picture of
Constable Country' *The Sunday Times*; Gavin Young,
Slow Boat to China, Century-Hutchinson.

ACKNOWLEDGEMENTS

Nothing is new. And little in this book is novel. What I have done is to apply ideas and techniques which are current in the literature on writing. I have drawn on the particularly extensive compilation of heuristic techniques for writing found in Jane B. Hughey, Deanna R. Wormuth, V. Faye Harfiel and Holly L. Jacobs (1983) *Teaching ESL Composition: Principles and Techniques*, Rowley, Mass.: Newbury House. A stimulating influence has been Donald M. Murray (1968) *A Writer Teaches Writing: A Practical Method of Teaching Composition*, Boston: Houghton Mifflin. It would also be an omission not to mention the influence of Linda Flowers and John R. Hayes, whose many articles, such as 'A cognitive process theory of writing' in *College English and Communication*, 32/4:365–87, have opened up new ways of looking at writing. There are also other materials writers who have been drawn on, either consciously or unknowingly. Among them are A. R. B. Etherton, whose *Mastering Modern English*, published in 1965 (Longman) incorporates a number of the heuristic techniques described in Hughey *et al.*, and Christopher Turk and John Kirkman (1982) *Effective Writing*, London: E & F Spoon. I should also like to thank Sue Krisman, novelist, for introducing me to the mini-saga and other interesting ways of tackling creative writing. Finally, I should like to thank my wife, Nora, for her unfailing encouragement and support and my son, Damon, for supervising the printing out of the manuscript from the word processor. Any omissions or errors must, alas, remain my own.

CONTENTS

FOREWORD

This series covers the four skill areas of Listening, Speaking, Reading and Writing at four levels — elementary, intermediate, upper-intermediate and advanced. Although we have decided to retain the traditional division of language use into the 'four skills', the skills are not treated in total isolation. In any given book the skill being dealt with serves as the *focus* of attention and is always interwoven with and supported by other skills. This enables teachers to concentrate on skills development without losing touch with the more complex reality of language use.

Our authors have had in common the following principles, that material should be:

- creative — both through author-creativity leading to interesting materials, and through their capacity to provoke creative responses from students;
- interesting — both for their cognitive and affective content, and for the activities required of the learners;
- fluency-focused — bringing in accuracy work only in so far as it is necessary to the completion of an activity;
- task-based — rather than engaging in closed exercise activities, to use tasks with pay-offs for the learners;
- problem-solving focused — so as to engage students in cognitive effort and thus provoke meaningful interaction;
- humanistic — in the sense that the materials speak to and interrelate with the learners as real people and engage them in interaction grounded in their own experience;
- learning-centred — by ensuring that the materials promote learning and help students to develop their own strategies for learning. This is in opposition to the view that a pre-determined content is taught and identically internalized by all students. In our materials we do not expect input to equal intake.

By ensuring continuing consultation between and among authors at different levels, and by piloting the materials, the levels have been established on a pragmatic basis. The fact that the authors, between them, share a wide and varied body of experience has made this possible without losing sight of the need to pitch materials and tasks at an attainable level while still allowing for the spice of challenge.

There are three main ways in which these materials can be used:

- as a supplement to a core course book;
- as self-learning material. Most of the books can be used on an individual basis with a minimum of teacher guidance, though the interactive element is thereby lost.
- as modular course material. A teacher might, for instance, combine intermediate *Listening* and *Speaking* books with upper-intermediate *Reading* and elementary *Writing* with a class which had a good passive knowledge of English but which needed a basic grounding in writing skills.

INTRODUCTION TO THE TEACHER

Aims of this material

This material is intended to develop composition skills rather than to focus on aspects of language. The composition skills concerned include:

- producing ideas
- identifying a purpose
- identifying a theme or mood
- developing a thesis or central idea
- organizing and reorganizing ideas
- taking account of the reader's knowledge and abilities
- developing paragraph organization
- indicating the connection and interrelationship of ideas
- choosing and using the most effective forms of expression
- checking and improving.

Methodology

Traditionally, students have been encouraged to mimic a model text, which is usually presented and analysed at an early stage. In this book, the model text is usually introduced after the students have tried to do a piece of writing first. The model text then becomes a resource against which to compare their own version and from which they can improve what they have written.

Another feature of the methodology is that the students work collaboratively on a lot of the activities, making use of pair and group work in a way which is increasingly common in the general language classroom. Such discussion is important in generating and organizing ideas and in discovering what it is that the writer wants to say, even though the actual writing may be done individually.

Students are also invited to exchange their compositions so that they become readers of each other's work. This is an important part of the writing experience because it is by responding as readers that students will develop an awareness of the fact that a writer is producing something to be read by someone else.

Finally, a practical point: using slips of paper and cards is better than writing everything on full page sheets during the idea-generating and organizing stages. Slips of scrap paper, scissors and glue sticks are all useful writing tools.

Stages

Most units are based on a similar sequence of activities:

1 getting ideas by brainstorming and discussion
2 writing ideas in note form
3 organizing ideas
4 writing a draft
5 improving the draft
6 writing a final draft
7 exchanging and reading each other's work.

Below is a suggested organization for using Unit 7, 'Developing a theme,' which is one of the longest units. This plan assumes two long sessions, each of two double periods. The fact is that writing requires time if it is to be done properly, but because the methods used in this material require a lot of student : student interaction, the class time given to 'writing' lessons will involve a lot of other productive use of language and so should not be seen as 'a waste of time'.

Homework preparation	*Classwork & discussion*
Session 1	
Introduction	
Section 2 Task 1	
	Task 2
	Introduction to Task 3
Task 3 completion	
Task 4	Task 4 pair work
	Task 5
	Task 6
Session 2	
Section 3 Task 1	Task 1 pair work
	Task 2
	Task 3
Task 4	
Task 5	Task 5 pair work

Task 6—revised and polished essay to be submitted to teacher for marking. The final draft can be done as homework.

The units are not uniform in length because some types of writing and the composition processes involved require more space and time and different techniques than others. As indicated above, some of the exercises can be done as homework, either as preparation or as follow-up to classwork. However, exercises intended for pair and group work should be handled as such in class.

Individual units

The organization and procedures to be followed have been made as explicit as possible in the rubrics for each exercise. The interpretation of these is open to each user. In particular, different users may decide to focus on additional aspects of the task; or they may introduce other ideas and material.

It is important to realize that the model texts have not been 'squeezed dry', either for content, organization or language so that there is room for variation in the work that can be based on them.

In general, most of the work is to be done by the students rather than by the teacher, the teacher's role being to advise on procedures and to monitor the work that is going on. The shift from pair and group to whole class mode may be made when it is judged to be appropriate or useful, and this will depend very much on how the students respond to the activities.

Correcting written work

Focus on global rather than local errors. That is, attend to errors which interfere with communication and comprehensibility rather than with errors which have little effect on the reader's ability to understand. In general, global errors involve poor organization, omitting needed information, misuse (including omission) of sentence linkers and logical connectors, breakdown in tense concord across sentences, ambiguity of article and pronoun reference (including relative pronouns), and general sentence and paragraph organization.

Teachers should not attempt to deal with all errors, but should focus on those which cause most difficulty to a reader. Errors may be indicated by underlining, and the student should attempt to work out the error and the correction. Student to student discussion in which they compare and correct errors can be helpful.

Another technique is to take a section of a student's text and to rewrite it. The rewritten version can then be distributed to the class together with the original, and a comparison can be made between the two versions. Alternatively, the teacher or another writer can do the writing assignment and a copy of his or her text can be issued to the students for comparison with their own version. Some very fruitful discussion can emerge from such comparisons, which will deal not simply with matters of expression, but with the ideas, the ways in which different texts have been organized and the viewpoint adopted by the writers.

Assessing work can be helped by using a banded marking scheme, as suggested by Hughey, Wormuth, *et al.* in *Teaching ESL Composition: Principles and Techniques*. They outline an 'ESL Composition Profile', with the following categories and mark allocations.

Categories	*Mark allocation out of 100%*
Content	13 to 30
Organization	7 to 20
Vocabulary	7 to 20
Language use	5 to 25
Mechanics	2 to 5

Each category receives a proportion of marks out of a total of 100, as shown above. A piece of writing is given marks in each category, so that, for instance, something which has excellent content would score between 27 and 30 in this category, whereas poor content would score a mark in the range 17 to 21. And so on within each category.

Such banded categories are helpful to both teacher and student, as they provide a more detailed form of feedback to the student than a single mark or grade. They also show the teacher in which respects a student is weak and in what ways work is improving during the writing course. You may find it useful to adapt such a scheme to your own purposes and to inform students about it so that they know the criteria being used for assessing their written work.

Conclusion

Writing is a discovery process. It involves discovering ideas, discovering how to organize them, and discovering what it is that you want to put over to your reader. So, a lot of what a writer does as a writer doesn't actually appear on the page. It is my hope that in using this material you will be able to develop some of the things which go on inside the writer's head because, most crucially, writing is a thinking process.

1 Introduction

Although writing usually involves writing by one person for another, learning to write may be better if several people work and talk together before, during and after writing. By doing so, we can help each other to understand the thinking and composing processes which are a most important part of writing.

In the activities which follow in this and other units, you will frequently be asked to work together. Such collaboration is an important feature of the work, and should not be omitted. If you are used to thinking about writing as something you do alone in silence, you may be pleasantly surprised by how much you learn by working and talking together with other people.

2 Different types of writing

Task 1

In fact, you already know a great deal about writing. As a reader you know what different types of writing look like, how ideas are organized and how they are appropriately expressed. As a writer, you know about some of the problems and solutions involved in writing.

With a partner, study the text below and those on pages 2 and 3 and classify them according to type.

Text 1

Thinking and talking about writing

Text 2

REPORT ON SPECIALIST TOUR TO INDONESIA

12th to 28th April 1985

R V White, Centre for Applied Language Studies
University of Reading

Introduction

The tour was undertaken in order to run two one-week writing workshops at
the universities of Andalas (Padanga, West Sumatra) and Udayana (Denpasa,
Bali). The workshops were to be attended by university and IKIP (training
college) teachers, and the intention was to introduce them to current
practics in the teaching of writing. A selection of textbooks was to be
provided for use on the workshop, and each university was to receive a
set at the completion of the week. In addition to the two workshops, I was
to visit the Police Science College in Jakarta. Two staff from there are
attending the Diploma in General and Applied Linguistics course at CALS
during the present session.

I will deal with each centre separately, and will conclude with some
general remarks relevant to my findings.

Universitas Andalas, Padang 15–19 April 1985.

<u>Purpose</u>

An outline of the workshop and a statement of objectives appears as
Appendix I. Copies of the outline were given to participants in advance
of the workshop.

<u>Participants</u>

The majority participants were staff of the University. However, the
University had been kind enough to invite teachers from the IKIP as well
as the local Muslim university. Twenty-three people attended regularly
throughout the week, while one or two staff members (including a lady from
the Indonesian Department) attended as and when their other commitments
permitted. A list of participants is given as Appendix II.

<u>Teaching: The Timetable</u>

The daily timetable was arranged as follows:

0800–1000	
1000–1030	'Snack'
1030–1300	
1300–1400	Lunch
1400–1530	
1530–1600	'Snack'
1600–1700	

1

Text 3

Audi Volkswagen

V.A.G (United Kingdom Limited)

Registered Office:
Yeomans Drive Blakelands Milton Keynes MK14 5AN
Telephone: (0908) 679121 Telex: 826448

30 September 1985

John Peters
18 Kendal Street
Reading   RG1 5DF

PS/ST/TOD/47B9

B633GAN

Dear Volkswagen Owner

<u>POSSIBLE DAMAGE TO BRAKE HOSES</u>

We would inform you that the vehicle bearing the above
registration number is one of a series of vehicles on which,
under unfavourable circumstances, cracks can appear in the
outer rubber covering of the brake hoses during operation.
In extreme cases, these cracks could lead to the hoses
leaking and thereby the failure of one or the other of the
two brake circuits, if the cracks are unnoticed over a long
period.

For safety reasons therefore it is considered necessary for
your vehicle to be subjected to a check. This check and any
necessary repairs are of course free of charge.

Please arrange to take your vehicle as soon as possible to
any V.A.G Dealer, taking this letter with you.

It would be appreciated if you will inform us if the vehicle
is not in your care. Please return this letter with the
name and address of the current user or owner to the
undersigned.

We would like to apologise for any inconvenience caused.

Yours sincerely

T J O'Donoghue
Service Technical Manager

V·A·G

Registered in England No 514809
A wholly owned subsidiary of Lonrho Plc

Text 4

Ques. No.

place for normal control.

The main control principle is feedback. In a living organism this is usually negative i.e by some mechanism secretion of a substance causes inhibition of the stimulus which is initiating its secretion. The ~~secretion~~ feedback (and initial stimulus) may ~~be the~~ nervous or endocrinal. The essential feature is that the feedback mechanism causes the right substance to be secreted at the right place at the right time, in ~~it is sensitive to the~~ the necessary quantity. It is sensitive to changes in the amount of secretion, e.g when there is much food in the stomach the gastric juice will be most needed, and so it will be used up faster and gastric will again be secreted as the inhibition by the gastric juice will not be as great.

Usually there are many factors influencing the activities of a part, and many forms of feedback mechanism, each sensitive to a slightly different thing. In the control of breathing, for example, the brain cells are sensitive to a rise in CO_2 in the blood while the carotid glomi are sensitive to a fall

Do not write in this margin

Text 5

Text 6

The Commandant,
Members of the Directing Staff and Students of the
Police Staff College, Bramshill
request the pleasure of the Company of

MR. & MRS. R. WHITE

at dinner on Thursday 14th November 1985.

R.S.V.P. The Commandant.
The Police Staff College,
Bramshill,
Nr. Basingstoke, Hampshire,
RG27 0JW

6.30 p.m. for 7 p.m. precisely
Dress: Dinner Jacket or Mess Dress
(miniature medals may be worn)
Ladies: Long dresses optional

Complete the table. You should briefly say what features of each text enabled you to classify it. These features include:

format: the way the text is set out on the page
graphics: typeset, typewritten or handwritten
style: formal, informal, casual.

Text	Type	Features
1		
2		
3		
4		
5		
6		

Task 2

Which of the text types that you studied in Task 1 do *you* write?

With a partner, discuss and then answer the following questions. Make notes of your discussion.

- How much writing do you do?
- What types of writing do you do? e.g. notes, messages, postcards, personal letters, business correspondence, academic papers, exam answers, imaginative writing, etc.
- What topics do you write about? e.g. travel, business affairs, academic topics in various subjects, recent activities, etc.
- What is the purpose of your writing? All of it will be to inform someone of something. Is your purpose:
  to tell them how to do something
  to describe something
  to report on events
  to persuade
  to entertain?
- Who receives and reads your writing? e.g. friends, colleagues, teachers, members of the public, etc.

  When you and your partner have finished your discussion, join with another pair and compare notes. What do you all have in common?

Task 3

One point which may have come up in your discussion is how difficult it is to write. The difficulty of writing depends on a number of things. In your group, discuss the following points and keep notes of your discussion.

- What are the most difficult types of writing that you have to do?
- Why are these pieces of writing so difficult?
- How do you try to overcome these difficulties?
- Are you always successful? (Be honest!)
- What steps do you go through before, during and after writing?
- How many attempts do you make before you are satisfied with what you have written? (Be honest!)

If you need some inspiration for your discussion, read the article on page 6 by Jeffrey Archer. The account is organized under the following headings, which you could use to give shape to your own discussion:

Timespan
Research
Location
Distractions
Routine
Technique
Final draft.

A blue pen, sharp pencil and then a Pimms

Can't type, but can edit on his secretary's word processor.

JEFFREY ARCHER, 44, author of four best sellers and the current British No 1 *First Among Equals.* Married with two sons.

Timespan: "It takes me two years from idea to publication. But actually writing the first draft lasts from six to eight weeks.

"Like Charles Dickens I don't know what I'm writing until I've written it. I never produce a synopsis before I start. Even my publisher doesn't know more than a brief outline before the manuscript is plonked on his desk."

Research: "I research people rather than things. For my latest book I had a long session with the Attorney General on electoral law and the Chief Whip took me round his Downing Street office.

"For *The Prodigal Daughter* I lunched with a senior White House official who then showed me round the Situation Room. The President can press a button and locate on a map every US and enemy submarine in the world.

"A little boy wrote to me once complaining that it was impossible for someone to fold a map (or any piece of paper) eight times. He was right. I hadn't done my research thoroughly!"

Location: "I used to write in Barbados, but the black situation got difficult. I now rent a house on the Bahamas. I seem to get inspiration staring at the sea and the beach."

Distractions: "Any background noise throws me. I have to get away from people. The phone goes with a tempting invitation to play cricket or the children want me to entertain them. The golden rule is no socializing. Writing is a full-time job."

Routine: "I rise at 6.30 am, have an hour's walk round the 18-hole golf course. I plan all the day's work then.

"After a light breakfast I write from 8 am to 10.30 am, doing about 1,500 words. I then take some more exercise, read the papers, have an early salad lunch and lie down for an hour. At 2 pm I spend a very painful, boring but necessary two hours re-writing what I've just done.

"By now it has expanded to 2,000 words. While the secretary is typing, I take another walk as the fresh air clears my head. I have a final scan over the pages, marking things with a pencil, give the corrected pages to the typist and take my first luxury of the day − a Pimms No 1.

"I eat a decent-sized supper alone − perhaps a lobster or steak − and am asleep by 10 pm."

Technique: "Before I start everything must be neatly laid out on my desk. Writing is like running a marathon. Therefore you must be completely relaxed. I can't type and so the secret of my success is a blue Tempo pen and a sharp German HB pencil. I only write on foolscap Oxford pads."

Final draft: "After the Bahamas I return home and try desperately to forget about the book for six weeks. I then go through the manuscript putting red dots on points that still need checking. While writing you must never stop the flow. You must keep going as you can always look things up later."

Task 4

Work in a group of five or six. Combine your experiences and the ideas discussed in Tasks 2 and 3 and make a summary of your discussion. Plan and write a group report to be entitled 'Thinking about writing'.

The report should be brief, clearly organized and to the point. It is to be read aloud by a representative of your group to the rest of the class. When each group has read its report, discuss the points that have been made. Is there a common theme to what has been said? What problems and solutions have been presented? What new ideas have you learnt?

Finally, make a list of six 'Helpful hints to writers' that you would give to anyone, based on the ideas that have come up in the work you have done in this unit. Then compare your helpful hints with the ideas given in the next section.

3   Helpful hints to writers

Although many people share similar writing problems and solutions, there are no universal recipes for successful writing because everyone is different. Even so, there are some procedures which most people will find useful some of the time.

Before writing

Brainstorm, if possible with other people. That is, think about the topic and purpose of writing and simply note down as many different ideas as you can in any order. Don't try to organize the ideas at this stage. (It is quite a good idea to write ideas on slips of papers or file cards so that you can easily organize and add to them later on.)

Whenever you want to generate ideas for a writing assignment, you can also use the questions given below and on page 8. The 'X' in each question stands for the topic, so you substitute the topic (e.g. 'travel', 'tradition', 'religion') for the X in each question. Obviously, not all questions can be used for all topics, while some questions can be applied to more than one.

	Questions	*Function*
1	What does X mean?	Define
2	How can X be described?	Describe
3	What are the component parts of X?	Analyse
4	How is X made or done?	Analyse the process
5	How *should* X be made or done?	Recommend
6	What is the essential function of X?	Analyse the function
7	What are the causes of X?	Analyse the causes
8	What are the consequences of X?	Analyse the outcome
9	What are the types of X?	Classify

	Questions	*Function*
10	How does X compare with Y?	Compare
11	What is the present status of X?	Compare
12	How can X be interpreted?	Interpret
13	What are the facts about X?	Report
14	How did X happen?	Narrate
15	What kind of person is X?	Characterize
16	What is my personal response to X?	Reflect
17	What is my memory of X?	Reminisce
18	What is the value of X?	Evaluate
19	How can X be summarized?	Summarize
20	What case can be made *for* or *against* X?	Argue

Organize the ideas you have noted down. Put them into groups according to topic, sequence or some other system. If you have written points on slips of paper or cards, this organization stage is easier to do than if you have written them on a single sheet of paper.

Think of further questions which your ideas give rise to or which they do not answer. Write them down.

Think of the information you now have in relation to these three questions:

- What do I know about the topic?
- What does my reader already know about the topic?
- What does my reader need or want to know about the topic?

It is what your reader does not know which you will have to give most attention to. But, you will also need to begin with what you and your reader share before introducing new information.

Find sources of information if you need further ideas and content to answer some of the questions you have raised. This may mean going to the library or searching through books and magazines at home.

During writing

Step one

Begin writing a first draft.

Concentrate on ideas and content rather than on expression. Refer to the ideas and notes from the previous stage. Don't worry about grammar and vocabulary at this stage.

If you are writing in a foreign language, use your own language for odd words and expressions when you can't think of them in the foreign language.

Step two

Try to read your draft from your reader's viewpoint. Do you need to add more information to help your reader? Have you begun with knowledge which you and your reader share in common before introducing new information?

Reorganize your draft by changing the order of ideas, paragraphs or sections. Use whatever means you find most useful for this purpose. Sometimes scissors and glue are useful, enabling you to cut up the draft and relocate sections easily.

At this stage, you may want to find an example of the type of writing you are doing to see how someone else handled the same writing task. In particular, it may be helpful to see how someone else organized the writing. You should not, of course, simply copy what someone else has written, as this will not actually help you to develop your own skill as a writer.

Step three

Focus on expression and accuracy. Translate into English any of the words or phrases you wrote in your own language.

Find alternative words if you find that you are repeating the same words or phrases too often. A thesaurus or a lexicon is useful as a source of alternative words. Unlike a dictionary, a thesaurus is organized by concept or topic. So, if you already have a word, but want to find alternatives, you can look up your original word and find numerous other choices in the thesaurus.

Write your second draft, incorporating improvements and corrections.

If you can, give the draft to someone else and read each other's drafts. Discuss the drafts and suggest improvements. The improvements may require you to:

- make your introduction more interesting or helpful
- change the order of ideas (and paragraphs)
- add further information to make things clear to your reader
- provide examples and details of general points
- make the relationship of linked ideas explicit
- cut out repetitious information
- combine ideas into a more economical form
- provide a clearer and more forceful conclusion which really does tie your ideas together.

Step four

Write a final version incorporating any changes or improvements suggested during the discussion with your partner.

Incubation

At any stage in the above sequence, you can — indeed, you should — give yourself some incubation time. This means putting aside the writing task and doing something else for an hour, a day, a week. Then return to the writing task. You may be surprised to find that a lot of good ideas have developed (or incubated) during the period when you weren't thinking about writing. For this reason, you should never leave a writing assignment to the last minute. Good writing, like much good cooking, requires time.

Conclusion

All of this may seem like a lot of work. In fact, writing does require more effort than speaking. However, it is as well to remember that, unlike most things we say, anything that we write is permanent. We are judged by what we write. With important writing (such as a business letter or report, an academic paper), it is vital that we take some trouble over what we write. To this end, we should not feel shy about discussing a piece of writing with a friend or a colleague — many good writers do this and even very successful writers (like Jeffrey Archer) are not afraid of asking people for advice on how to improve their writing. Nor should we feel that we are poor writers if we have to write something several times — most things that we read are actually the final product of much rewriting.

Finally, writing really does improve with practice. So, even though writing is partly inspiration, that is, having good ideas at the right time, it is also the result of application. And application can involve using some of the procedures which you yourselves have suggested as well as the techniques outlined in the 'Helpful hints' section and in the other units in this book.

1 Introduction

Stories can be told in pictures or in words. The cartoon tells a story in pictures. As in most stories there is a sequence of events, at least one actor or character and a setting. The story has a beginning, development and an ending. And, as in most stories, there is a point or theme which the story illustrates. When we look at the cartoon, we recognize that the events shown there tell us something about human behaviour generally.

In this unit we are going to work on ways of telling stories about journeys. In other words, we are going to put things in order. And we are going to see how even a story of a journey can be used to develop a theme or to make a point. We will begin with a text which has more order than story; and then we will go on to texts which combine order with a story and a theme.

2

Putting things in order

OXFAM

BRETECHER

2   Narrating events

Task 1

Text 1 is a non-linear text; that is, it is not presented in lines of printed words and sentences as in ordinary prose. Even though it is a non-linear text, it gives information which is organized on the same basis as similar information in a linear text.

Study Text 1. What is it?

Tick the questions which are answered by the text.

☐ When?   ☐ Why?   ☐ Where?
☐ How?   ☐ Who?   ☐ How long?

Tick the correct headings for the way the information is organized.

☐ by hierarchy   ☐ by sequence   ☐ by contrast
☐ by movement   ☐ by cause and effect ☐ by space

Does Text 1 tell a story? If not, what is missing?

Text 1

DATE	CITY AIRPORT	LOCAL TIME	FLIGHT	CLASS	STATUS
21 Mar	London (Heathrow) ar.	2000	SQ21	Y	OK
22 Mar	Singapore ar.	1830			
25 Mar	Singapore dep.	1445	SQ108	Y	OK
25 Mar	Kuala Lumpur ar.	1535			
04 Apr	Kuala Lumpur dep.	2030	SQ113	Y	OK
04 Apr	Singapore ar.	2120			
04 Apr	Singapore dep.	2230	SQ22	Y	OK
05 Apr	London (Heathrow) ar.	0645			

Task 2

An itinerary only gives the skeleton of the journey. There is a lot of information which is not given.

Make a list of what would be needed to turn Text 1 from an itinerary into a story. (You may find it useful to think of the information that you would like to know about the journey.) Compare your list with a partner's.

Task 3

You should now have two sets of items:

the information given in the itinerary
the extra information which you would like to know.

These could be combined and presented in a linear text as a story.

Write a story of an imaginary journey to Singapore and Kuala Lumpur. Your readers are other members of your class.

Use the information you have worked on as a basis for your story. Use your imagination — or if that fails, refer to books and travel brochures about Singapore and Malaysia to provide you with background information.

Organize your story by sequence and write between 300 and 500 words.

When you have finished, exchange stories with a partner. Read each other's stories and compare and discuss what you have written. Are your stories different? What makes them different?

Task 4

Text 2 is a linear text. Read it and decide in what ways it is similar to Text 1.
- How is Text 2 organized?
- Was Text 2 originally written or spoken? How can you tell?

Text 2

I was once (er) having to travel between two small towns in southern Turkey and I was given as guides by the local police a small party of men who were going with an empty string of mules to pick up some grapes and bring them back since the mules were empty they were able to take my gear and give me a lift too and (er) we bargained for a price it wasn't very much so we stopped in the evening after an afternoon's walk and I'd taken some tins of stuffed (er er) dolmas egg plants and some big water bottle and of course we sat down and I said please share my meal and of course they shared it and (er) then later in the night about midnight I was pretty tired by this time we came to a place where there were camp fires and one or two other caravans around and they said we're stopping for a meal and they said you can sleep over there so I went to sleep.

Task 5

Text 2 was originally spoken. While the speaker was talking, the story was recorded and then it was transcribed, that is, it was written down. The transcription is like the spoken text in that it has no punctuation. The beginnings and ends of sentences are not shown, and there is no punctuation for direct speech. The lack of punctuation makes it rather difficult to read at first.

Work with a partner and add punctuation to Text 2. You can read the text to each other and mark in the punctuation at agreed points in the transcript.

Task 6

Like most stories, Text 2 is organized sequentially, and as in many spoken anecdotes, the order of events is shown by sequencers and linkers, such as *and, then* and *next*.

Ring all the sequencers and linkers in Text 2. How many different ones are used?

Task 7

In a spoken anecdote, many speakers use a fairly limited range of sequencers and linkers. When we write, the repeated use of *and* or *so* or *then* is regarded as bad style. For this reason, we prefer to use a wider range of sequencers and linkers, such as these:

first next after that afterwards eventually
later next previously subsequently then finally lastly
meanwhile in the meantime

Rewrite Text 2 to make it read as a written text, using some of the sequencers listed above. (Keep your edited version of Text 2 as you will need it later.)

Task 8

Text 3 is another story of a journey. It is taken from a newspaper article and was obviously written to be read, unlike Text 2, which was originally spoken to be listened to.

Read it and compare it with Text 2.

- Apart from content, how do the two texts differ?
- Which text shows more variety in the way the story is told?

Text 3

'East Bergholt, Four Sisters,' called the bus driver.

I got out and looked around, but all I could see was the Colchester to Ipswich main road. Where was East Bergholt? Answer: more than a mile away. I'd wrongly assumed, when I read the timetable, that *all* bus stops listed under 'East Bergholt' would be in the village.

I began to walk, glad I was carrying only one nylon shoulder-bag, particularly as I also planned to walk from East Bergholt through Constable Country to Flatford Mill — nearly another mile. But before I'd gone more than a few yards, a kindly lady from East Bergholt offered me a lift.

Task 9

The writer, Jean Sargeant, has changed the order of events in her story from the way in which they actually occurred. This makes her version of the story more interesting than a simple, sequential report of events, which is the way the story-teller told his anecdote in Text 2. As a writer, Jean Sargeant has the opportunity to reconstruct events and to develop the organization of her story, and one of the ways she does this is to use the past perfect tense, for example:

I'd assumed (I had assumed)
I'd gone (I had gone).

Complete these sentences to show the actual sequence of events.

I . . . . the timetable.

I . . . . that all 'East Bergholt' bus stops were

in the village.

The driver . . . . 'East Bergholt'.

I . . . .

I . . . . around.

I was not in the village.

Compare the order of events as given in the story with the order of events as they actually occurred. Why does Jean Sargeant tell the events in the wrong order?

Return to your edited version of Text 2 and experiment with changes in sequence by using the past perfect tense as well as the past simple tense.

How many changes can you make? Do not make too many alterations, as they will confuse the reader. What is the effect of using one or two past perfects in the story?

3   Making a point

Task 1

Jean Sargeant began her story with a quotation and the first two paragraphs of her account tell the reader about the purpose and setting of her journey. Read the two opening paragraphs below.

- How does the quotation introduce one of the themes of the story?
- How does the writer continue the idea from the quotation into the second paragraph?
- How does the opening below differ from the beginning of Text 2?

'To travel hopefully is a better thing than to arrive and the true success is to labour,' wrote Robert Louis Stevenson in his essay *El Dorado*. A week's holiday spent travelling around Suffolk by local buses has almost converted me to his view.

The labour came first: I collected bus timetables, maps, guidebooks and spent days poring over them planning my route. Then I travelled hopefully by National Coach to Colchester, where I connected with the Eastern Counties bus network.

Beginning with a quotation can be an effective way of opening an essay. The quotation sets the theme — in this case, travel — and it should prepare the reader for the main ideas and general viewpoint of the writer.

Task 2

Later in her narrative, Jean Sargeant uses another way of showing the relationship of one event to another.

I *was going* back to the Four Sisters to stop *when I discovered* a better bus for my next destination, Ipswich. I didn't know its route, but part of the fun of a bus trip is the element of magical mystery tour: when the bus came, I just relaxed and enjoyed the Suffolk countryside through the windows.

How does the writer show the relationship between an event and the circumstances of or background to that event? The words in italic will give you a clue.

In addition to telling the reader what happened, the writer also comments upon events. That is, she tells the reader what she thinks or feels about events or experiences or circumstances.

What part of the text is narrative and what part is comment? Quote the actual words.

Task 3

A story of a journey would be dull if the writer didn't use some descriptive language. Jean Sargeant's title, 'Moving Picture of Constable Country', tells the reader to expect both a story of a journey and a description of the countryside, particularly as she travelled through a region of England associated with John Constable, the famous nineteenth-century landscape painter.

Here is another paragraph from the story. Underline and list all the descriptive words. Make a list of the things she saw.

Read the paragraph without the descriptive words. What is it like when these words are missing?

I went down to the docks and enjoyed an exhilarating walk along the quayside, almost deserted on a windy Saturday afternoon when derricks and cranes were idle against wide grey skies, and gulls swooped over choppy grey water. I found the handsome Old Customs House, was invited aboard a barge and stopped to look at a cargo boat. 'She's just come back from Spain,' an elderly man who was drawing told me.

Task 4

Here are two more paragraphs from near the end of the story. Underline all the descriptive language and make a list of the different things which the writer noticed.

Find the simile, that is, the expression that says that one thing is like another. How does the simile help to give the reader a clear picture of the scene?

Under overcast skies, grey waves murmured soothingly on the shingle beach. But a big orange-and-blue lifeboat stood poised like an exotic fish or bird; and the Elizabethan Moot Hall, once in the centre of the town, is now on the beach — the sea has swallowed the rest.
   I returned by way of Sudbury where, looking through the picture windows of the Mill Hotel, I watched a Constable landscape compose itself beneath big light-filled skies. Cows moved slowly through the lush water-meadows of the Stour and a child's jersey added the right touch of red. Then I bused to Lavenham, the show-piece 16th-century wool town with its timber buildings, Guildhall and Flemish weavers cottages.

Good descriptive writing depends on observation, that is, noticing things. As you can see from the list of things you have made in this and the previous task, Jean Sargeant noticed a lot of things. Some of them were quite small and unimportant, such as the child's jersey mentioned in paragraph 2 above. However, putting such small details together helps to give the reader a very vivid picture of the scene — rather like a sequence of pictures in a TV programme. Although each picture by itself is unimportant, in combination, the pictures evoke a rich impression of the landscape.

The writer also uses a useful type of sentence:

I went by way of X to Y where ...

In addition, she uses a very effective expression: *compose itself*. Using the reflexive pronoun in this way is useful with verbs like 'compose' and 'reveal' when describing a landscape, e.g.

I watched a Constable landscape compose itself beneath big light-filled skies.
The valley revealed itself as we passed out of the trees into the open countryside of the downs.

Using 'compose' is also very appropriate in Jean Sargeant's description because she was travelling through a region of England well known through Constable's landscape paintings. The use of the verb 'compose' establishes an association with the painter and reminds the reader of one of the themes of the story. The visual theme also helps to connect together the places through which Jean Sargeant passed and the experiences which she had on her journey.

Task 5

There is usually a reason for telling a story, whether it is a spoken anecdote or a written account of events. Jean Sargeant's story has two themes: travel itself and the Constable landscape of Suffolk. Her theme is connected to her purpose in telling the story, which was to let her readers know that travelling about Suffolk by public transport could be an interesting and enjoyable experience which they might care to try.

The lecturer used the story in Text 2 to illustrate the laws of hospitality which are part of the traditions of nomadic peoples in the Middle East. Having quoted a story to show how desert travellers would put up with considerable discomfort in order to share scarce food with other travellers, he then gives a counter example, which is the basis of the story in Text 2. Here is the rest of his anecdote as Text 4.

Text 4

I got nothing to eat and then after a while I felt a boot in my back said we're off so I got up and (er) it was desperately chilly and I decided to ride this donkey at this stage soon through the night I was praying for the sun to come up and I was putting on all the odd clothes I could get hold of and I was still shivering then the sun came up and then I was praying for it to go down equally desperately [laughter] I thought at any rate I've got a drop of water and about half way through the morning I reached for this cannister and of course they'd drunk it so (er) we eventually arrived at the township where we were coming to about mid-day I was by this time practically falling off the mule hanging round its neck and there were some children coming along and cheering ironically so I fell off and staggered on my feet [laughter] with what dignity I could muster and then finally we got to the caravan *sarai* and I asked for a bed and the leader of the caravan came along and demanded (er) extra subsidy for some reason because I'd ridden on his donkey or something and for once I had

the courage to answer him back in his own coin and I sent him away with
a flea in his ear [laughter] but (um) at any rate (um) don't judge all
nomadic travel by that particular experience I've had many other
occasions where everything was shared much more hospitably

In the story of her journey, Jean Sargeant added elements to show
the reader how she reacted to the things she saw and the
experiences she had. Similarly, in his anecdote, the story-teller adds
elements to the sequence of events to show his listeners how he felt
about what was happening:

I decided to ride this donkey
I was praying for the sun to come up
I thought at any rate I've got a drop of water
I staggered on my feet with what dignity I could muster

And he ends with two statements which remind his listeners of the
point of the story — that it was an illustration of a general principle he
was trying to make about the hospitality of nomadic travellers. If an
anecdote doesn't have a point, the listener or reader feels frustrated
or even annoyed and may react with the question 'So what?'

Complete the anecdote by converting Text 4 into written form and
adding it to the edited version of Text 2 which you prepared in earlier
tasks.

Provide a suitable opening and ending linked to the theme which the
story-teller has developed. The opening should arouse the interest of
the reader. The ending should refer to the point developed by the
story-teller.

You could begin the story in various ways.

Method	Example
Action	We stopped in the evening after . . .
General statement	Nomads are not always hospitable.
Proverb or quotation	'A man travels the world in search of what he wants and returns home to find it.' (George Moore)
	'He travels fastest who travels alone.' (Rudyard Kipling)
Direct speech	'We're stopping for a meal,' they said.

Vary the sequencing of events and develop the descriptive aspect of
the story.

Give the story an appropriate title.

Task 6

You should now be ready to write an essay of your own, combining narrative and description and comment, as in Jean Sargeant's article and in the anecdote about travel in southern Turkey. You can write about a tour or an excursion which you have done, or you can write about an imaginary journey as if you had done it.

1   Your reader is to be someone like yourself.
2   Plan an itinerary of your tour:

Sequence	Places	Activities

3   Choose an opening theme or quotation with which to start your story, and use the theme to connect together different parts of your essay.
4   Write the essay in several paragraphs, combining narrative (what you did) with description (what you saw) and comment (what or how you felt).
5   Use a variety of verbs of movement. Don't just repeat *went, travelled, walked.* Use a thesaurus or lexicon to find alternative and more precise terms.
6   Use a variety of ways of showing sequence and the relationship of one event to another.
7   Use a range of descriptive language to help give the reader a good picture of what you saw and felt. Again, a thesaurus or lexicon will help with the vocabulary.

Your composition should give the reader an interesting picture of the places and things that you saw — or that you imagined you saw. The reader should also be able to share some of your own feelings about the experiences you had.

Exchange essays with a partner and read each other's work. Discuss what you have written, how you organized it, and compare the way you developed your theme. Discuss ways in which you could have improved what you wrote.

1 Introduction

Many newspaper and magazine articles are based on interviews. The journalist records an interview with someone and then incorporates the material from the interview in an article. There is a great deal of skill in taking unedited spoken material and shaping it into an article which will be both interesting and readable. This unit is concerned with converting such spoken language into interesting and readable prose.

2 Changing spoken language into written language

Task 1

Read Text 1 which is part of an interview with a housewife whose husband had recently retired.

Text 1

Interviewer Mrs Tracey, I wonder if you could tell me a little bit about your routine — your sort of household routine.

Mrs Tracey Well, in the morning — er — I have to tell you that my husband goes out quite early, but before he goes out he does bring me a cup of tea, which is always very welcome, and then I get up about — er — quarter to eight. But now of course I'll get up a little earlier because I have someone staying in the house. And then I go down and I have some breakfast and clear up the breakfast things and start tidying up generally and then usually start cooking — either I, one day I might be baking bread and making cakes, making jam, doing something like that and — er — then we have a lunch about — a light snack about half past twelve. And I always take a rest in the afternoon, now, and then usually go out for a walk.

Interviewer Do you have a dog?

Mrs Tracey No, no, well my husband likes walking, you see. We go . . .

Mr Tracey She has me!

Mrs Tracey We very often go out walking together and — hmm — sometimes I go up to the shops to buy some odd little thing but usually do our shopping, a big shopping, all at once. My husband takes me in the car and . . .

Interviewer Where do you do your main shopping? Sainsbury's, or . . .?

Mrs Tracey No, Waitrose was our main shopping centre, really, isn't it? We still go there, although we've got an Asda as you know.

Interviewer Yes, yes.

Mrs Tracey Down Earley and sometimes we go down there now, but — er, er — we still like Waitrose very much.

Mr Tracey In Woodley.

Mrs Tracey In Woodley.

Interviewer Yes, and when would you do that, on Saturdays normally?
Mrs Tracey No, no, we try not to do it Saturdays because they get very busy. We do it odd times, don't we?

Apart from the way the interview is set out, there are a number of features of the language which clearly show that Text 1 is a transcript of natural spoken language. The speakers were not reading from a script. They were making up — or improvising — as the interview proceeded.

Identify three things which show that Text 1 was originally spoken language. Compare your ideas with a partner's. Discuss the features you have found and why you chose them.

Task 2

Obviously, to change this interview into something readable, quite a few changes would have to be made. The first change is to turn the language from spoken language into written language. This does not mean simply rewriting it as reported speech, as other changes will be necessary.

With a partner, discuss what changes you would make to the language of Text 1. Rewrite part of Text 1 in written style.

Compare your version with a version written by another pair. Discuss the changes you have made and any differences between your two versions.

Task 3

Apart from the language, there is also the question of content. Improvised spoken language tends to be very redundant, that is, speakers tend to say more than is necessary for a written version of the same message. To help listeners understand, speakers often repeat themselves, or say something in more than one way. Such repetition or redundancy is not good written style.

Cross out — that is, edit any redundant items in Text 1. Compare your editing with that of a partner and discuss any differences. Combine your changes in an agreed version.

You should now have a much briefer and tidier version of Text 1, but it will still not be in a form appropriate for presenting to a reader — especially a magazine reader.

Task 4

Let us assume that the interview with Mrs Tracey is going to be published as an article entitled 'A day in the life of Edwina Tracey'. The article is one of a regular series in which people talk about their routines and way of life. The articles are all based on interviews, but the material from the interviews has to be edited.

Write about Mrs Tracey's routine, using the edited material from Text 1. Write in the first person so that the article still gives the impression that it is Mrs Tracey who is speaking.

When you have finished, compare your version with that of a partner. Discuss any differences and explain why you wrote yours the way you did.

Task 5

Text 2 is a magazine article from a series which has been running in *The Sunday Times* for many years. The series is called 'A life in the day of'. Over the years, hundreds of people have described their life — not only their daily routine, but also other aspects of their work and leisure, their tastes, habits and activities. Thus the title — 'A life in the day of . . .'.

Text 2 is part of a longer article 'A life in the day of Kathy Coulter' who was, at the time, an Oxford undergraduate and, during her spare time, a successful fashion model.

Text 2

A LIFE IN THE DAY OF KATHY COULTER

 Work at Oxford is based around one or two weekly tutorials. At your tutorial you read out your essay, and then they give you a title or a subject for the next week — normally something quite general like 'Write about Comedy in Joyce' or 'How universal an author is Hardy?'. I normally work in the college library except if I'm reading a novel, when I like to read lying on my bed. Sometimes for a change I go to the Bodleian Library where there's a lovely atmosphere, especially in the Radcliffe Camera.

Lunch is rather hurried, just grabbing a meal — it's not a terribly big social occasion. Teatime is quite social but it's nicest in the summer because we bring everything out into the quad and have tea on the grass. I don't usually eat dinner in hall because it's a three-course meal and terribly fattening and I have to watch my weight. I hate to stand on a weighing machine so I judge it by the holes in my belt.

Compare 'A life in the day of Kathy Coulter' with what you wrote about Mrs Tracey's routine. What differences are there?

Obviously, there will be differences in content — Ms Coulter is a young, unmarried student whereas Mrs Tracey is a middle-aged housewife. There will probably be important differences in style between your description and the article on Ms Coulter.

How has the journalist managed to edit the interview with Ms Coulter while at the same time retaining the impression of someone talking?

Task 6

To see how the journalist might have worked, we really need a transcript of the original interview. Unfortunately, this is not available. However, it is possible to improvise a version of the interview.

With a partner, one of you take the role of interviewer, while the other take the role of Ms Coulter. Using the content of the second paragraph, record the interview.

Transcribe the recording and compare it with Text 2. What differences are there?

Edit the transcript and then compare your edited version with the published version in Text 2.

Task 7

To obtain information about someone's life and routine, it is necessary to interview them. This means preparing some questions.

With a partner, write out ten questions you would ask someone in order to find out about his or her life and routine.

Find another partner, and use the questions for an interview. If you can, record the interview and then transcribe it. If you cannot record it, take full notes of what your partner says in reply to your questions.

Edit the transcript and your notes and finally, write the description of your partner's life and routine, under the title '*A life in the day of (name)*'.

When you have written the description, show it to your partner so that he or she can comment on it.

3   Using anecdotes to make a point

Task 1

Telling stories and anecdotes is an important feature of conversation. Stories are also the basis of much reporting. Often an anecdote is used to illustrate or to make a point.

Text 3 is an example of a spoken anecdote. (The [laughter] is from the audience.) It comes from a lecture on nomads, i.e. groups of people who wander in search of pasture for their animals. The lecturer has just discussed the 'sanctity of the road' which means that if anybody is attacked on the road, it is not just a crime but a sin.

Read Text 3. What point does the lecturer make in the anecdote?

Text 3

These people for whom in many respects I have a great regard are slightly less respectful to their travellers and to the sanctity of the road — ah — a friend of mine who spent some time in that country just after the First World War and before it too for that matter told me that once he was travelling along a road with a local guide and they came to a pile of stones recently put there which was clearly a grave and — er — normally in these circumstances this means somebody who has been found dead on or near the road so he asked his guide if he knew the story behind this grave and began to laugh and said yes he did as it happened it was a very funny story and — er — [laughter] he would tell it — what happened he said was that there was — er — a shepherd pasturing his flocks around here and two men came along and one said to the other I bet that fellow's got some money on him let's — er — waylay him and they started firing at him but he began firing back from behind that rock and they couldn't really get him but then one of the men said to the other you keep him covered and I'll sneak around through that low ground and get up behind him behind that rock up there and catch him in the back and he said he did this and he shot him and they robbed him and they buried him there so my friend said you seem to know an awful lot about this — naturally said the storyteller I was the man behind the rock [laughter]

Task 2

This transcript is quite difficult to read because it lacks sentence boundaries and punctuation.

With a partner, identify the sentence boundaries and the direct and reported speech. (To do this, you may find it helpful to read sections of the anecdote aloud to each other.) Punctuate the transcript.

Give the anecdote a title. It should reflect the point which the teller of the anecdote intends to make.

Task 3

An anecdote has a structure or organization. Like all narratives, it has a sequence — a beginning, a middle and an end. But an anecdote also has a point or thesis which the story-teller wishes to make. A thesis answers the question, 'So what?' If an anecdote doesn't answer this question, it lacks a point and the listener or reader will feel dissatisfied. So, one of the first things which you should remember when telling an anecdote is that it should have a point and if your reader finishes with the question 'So what?' unanswered, you will have failed.

In an anecdote, the 'punch-line' — that is, the climax of the story — will usually be delayed right to the end. If the hearer or reader is given the climax first, then much of the interest of the anecdote will be lost. Even if the hearer or reader can guess what the conclusion will be, he or she will want to listen or read to the end to confirm this guess.

The structure of anecdotes is thus quite different from reports (Unit 11), in which the main points are usually presented first, with supporting detail to follow.

With a partner, identify the main parts of the anecdote in Text 3.

- Which part is:

  the introduction
  the development of the story
  the punch-line or climax?
- What is the thesis or point of the story?
- What difference would it have made if the lecturer had begun like this?

Once a friend of mine met a man who had broken the sanctity of the road by killing and robbing a shepherd who had been pasturing his flocks near the road.

Task 4

The anecdote in Text 2 is essentially a spoken story, even with correct punctuation. To incorporate this anecdote in an essay, changes would have to be made to it.

With a partner, discuss the changes which would be necessary.

- Would you make changes of:

  grammar
  vocabulary
  style
  organization?
- In what kind of essay and on what topic could you use the anecdote?
- What point or thesis could you illustrate with the anecdote?

Write a short essay and include an edited version of the anecdote to illustrate the thesis of your composition. (You could begin your essay with the anecdote, or you could include it in the body of the essay.) Presumably, your essay will have something to do with travel and the morality of travellers. However, you may have decided that the anecdote would be better used in an essay in which you wish to illustrate another quite different point.

Task 5

Anecdotes are often used during informal discussions when a speaker wishes to entertain or to make a point.

Try to record such an anecdote. You may record one from a television or radio programme. So-called 'chat' shows often include anecdotes told by one of the people on the show. Alternatively, you may prefer to collect an anecdote from conversation with friends. Ask their permission to record the conversation!

Edit the anecdote and incorporate it in an essay. Use the anecdote to illustrate or to make a relevant point. This means that your essay will have to be written round the anecdote and your theme will be derived from it.

Exchange essays with a partner and compare what you have written. Discuss why you wrote as you did and how you incorporated the anecdote in the essay.

Suggest ways of improving each other's essays.

4

Promoting an image

1 Introduction

The advertisement for Portugal on the opposite page emphasizes two aspects of tourism in Portugal. The theme of contrast is emphasized by the two pictures and the captions, one of each being upside down, thus creating a visual surprise for readers, whose attention will be gained long enough, possibly, for the advertiser's message to get through to them.

Complete the table below with the contrasts stated in the advertisement.

Aspect 1	Aspect 2
relaxing on beaches suntan in summer	being active in sport . . . . gambling in casinos . . . .

Such an advertisement is a reminder that there is more than one way of looking at anything — a product, a service, a country or a person. Much advertising is concerned with promoting images of people, services or products because advertising is not only about making something known to the public — it is also concerned with associating the goods or services with an image which will appeal to a particular consumer. Equally important, the image should be memorable.

Advertising agents and copy-writers are very skilled at developing images through the clever use of language and visual elements and, by such means, persuading consumers to buy goods and services. In this unit, you will have an opportunity to develop some of these skills, which are relevant whenever the purpose of writing is to attract attention, persuade the reader and create a memorable impression.

2 Using language persuasively

Task 1

Have you ever thought of advertising yourself? Why would you want to advertise yourself? What aspects of yourself — appearance, personality, habits, likes and dislikes — would you advertise? In other words, what image of yourself would you wish to promote?

One view of Portugal

another view of Portugal

In Portugal, you can laze on our golden beaches (or practice your favourite sport).

You can get a beautiful suntan in the summer (or in the spring, or autumn).

You can go fishing in our tranquil lakes (or you can try for bigger fish in our casinos).

You can dine simply on delicious fresh sardines (or you can go gourmet. We're in the Michelin Guide – lots of times).

In Portugal, you can find whatever holiday you want. Ask your travel agent for details, or send for a free brochure – we'll turn your ideas about Portugal upside down.

Portugal. A lot more holiday, for a lot less money.

AIR PORTUGAL

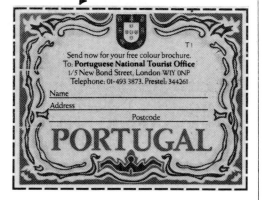

Send now for your free colour brochure.
To: **Portuguese National Tourist Office**
1/5 New Bond Street, London W1Y 0NP
Telephone: 01-493 3873. Prestel: 344261

Name _____

Address _____

Postcode _____

PORTUGAL

On separate pieces of paper, write down three reasons why you might want to advertise yourself. Under each reason, list those things about yourself that you would include in each advertisement.

Briefly describe the image of yourself which you would like to promote. To do this, make a list of adjectives. (You may find it helpful to refer to a thesaurus.)

Task 2

People advertise themselves for several reasons, such as:

offering a service, e.g. typing, driving, household repairs, etc.
offering themselves for employment,
asking for funds towards a company or venture
seeking sponsorship for an activity, such as exploration
seeking a companion, possibly with the idea of forming a relationship.

Such advertisements appear in the classified advertisements or 'small ads' section of newspapers. Some newspapers specialize in advertisements to the extent that they have no other content. Others, such as *The Times*, have 'Personal Columns', in which the following advertisements appeared.

Text 1

HISTORY GRADUATE. Numerate with clerical experience. Widely read and good communicator seeks Saturday/Sunday employment. Anything considered. Box No 1905L. The Times.

Text 2

SPANISH GIRL 23, grad Public Relations, good English, s/h. seeks exciting post from Sept. Tel. AMPARO 0902 759840.

Note the order in which the information is given in Text 2:

nationality
age
qualifications
job required
contact phone number/address.

Using the notes you made in Task 1, write an advertisement for yourself, in which you seek employment, either full or part time. The advertisement is to appear in the personal column of *The Times*.

Task 3

As you may have discovered, writing an advertisement about yourself isn't easy, even when you are advertising for something like a job. It is even more difficult if the advertisement is for a companion, and it is especially difficult if the companion is a prospective husband or wife!

What qualities would you wish to promote in an advertisement for yourself when seeking a companion? Make a list.

What qualities would you wish for in your companion? Make a list.

Write an advertisement, in which you promote your own image and in which you specify the characteristics of the companion you are looking for. The advertisement is to appear in the personal column of a newspaper.

Task 4

Text 3 is based on such an advertisement. What is wrong with it?

Text 3

> I am a sincere, English, unattached male, aged 47 and 5ft 8in tall. I am young looking and not unattractive. I have no ties, and I have my own house and car. I am reasonably financially secure. I am considered humourous, warm hearted, understanding and generous. I have many and varied interests. I wish to meet an intelligent, attractive female, aged between 30 and 40. Her status is unimportant, but a child is welcome. She should live within a 15 mile radius of East Croydon. I wish to meet her with a view to friendship and marriage. A photograph would be appreciated. All letters will be answered. Discretion is assured. Box 7811.

Did you find the style of Text 3 embarrassing? Why? Cross out all of the redundant items and rewrite Text 3.

Begin as follows:

> GENUINE
> Sincere, English, unattached male, 47, 5ft 8in, young looking . . .

Now compare your rewrite of Text 3 with the original. Which one is better? Why?

No doubt the most important change you made was to delete 'I'. The repetition of 'I' in Text 3 makes the advertiser seem very egocentric. Also, the first person is conventionally understood to be the subject of the advertisement, anyway, so making this explicit is unnecessary.

There is also another consideration — cost. To keep cost down, redundant items — including pronouns and many verbs — are usually omitted in such advertisements.

Check the advertisement you wrote in Task 2. Make any changes which you think will improve it in the light of the work you have done on Text 3.

Task 5

Describing your 'inner self' is the most difficult part of describing yourself. Elizabeth Tener, author of *Getting Personal*: *Finding that Special Someone Through The Classifieds* lists the following questions as a way of dealing with this difficulty.

- What elements of your appearance do you feel are most attractive?
- What achievements have you felt especially positive about in the past year?
- When friends and family members compliment you, what do they most often say?
- What skills or personal qualities do you usually bring to a party, a business meeting, an organization you're volunteering for, a family dinner?
- Which special abilities seem to emerge when you're solving a family crisis, cheering up a discouraged friend, getting yourself together after a personal disappointment?
- What do you think are your special contributions to the people around you?

Elizabeth Tener suggests that, after thinking about these questions, you make a two-column chart on a separate piece of paper. In the first column, put an adjective you feel describes you. In the second column, give two examples of how this quality usually shows up in your life. Keep your examples short (under ten words) and as lively and descriptive as possible.

Descriptive adjective	*Examples in my life*

The next task is to decide what combination of adjectives and examples will give the truest and most interesting portrait of you. If any of the adjectives seem weak, search through a thesaurus for a stronger one. A thesaurus contains lists of synonyms so that, for instance, under the entry *cheerful* you would find words such as *blithe, genial, sociable, optimistic, upbeat, happy-go-lucky*. Such synonyms might be better than the adjective that first came to mind.

Task 6

Write a final version of an advertisement about yourself. If you can, type it out. If you can't type it, print it neatly. Make sure that you are anonymous, that is, don't include your name in the advertisement.

Either
Bring your advertisement to class and put it together in a mixed collection with the advertisements written by other students. Select at random one of the other advertisements. Read it out to the rest of the class. Try to identify the person who wrote the advertisement.

or
Bring your advertisement to class and pin it on the classroom noticeboard, together with the advertisements of your classmates. Try to identify the 'advertiser' for each advertisement.

and
When you have identified the subject of the advertisement, discuss whether the image you had as a reader was the same as the image the writer intended to promote.

3 Developing a theme or mood

Task 1

When you advertised yourself, you wrote a classified advertisement. Another type of advertisement found in magazines and newspapers is the display advertisement, such as the one advertising Portugal on page 29. Display advertisements are a combination of text plus pictures.

In a group of three, prepare a display advertisement for a number of tropical islands which are a long way from anywhere else. Their only similarity with Portugal is the fact that both countries have beaches, so the Portuguese advertisement will not provide a particularly appropriate model for you except in being attention-getting, having a theme and ending with a good signature line:

Portugal. A lot more holiday, for a lot less money.

Decide on:

who your advertisement is aimed at
what image of the place you are going to promote
what illustration will accompany the text.

Refer to a thesaurus to find useful vocabulary. Check the references under such terms as the following:

special, memorable, notable, excellent, perfect, unique.

Write your advertisement in no more than 100 words. Try to end your advertisement with a good signature line.

Task 2

Read Text 4 which is the copy from an advertisement for the Seychelles and compare it with the advertisement which your group wrote.

In what ways does Text 4:

draw attention to itself
sustain interest
make itself memorable
create an image?

Text 4

Out of this world, but not out of your reach

A thousand miles from anywhere, in the heart of the Indian Ocean, lie the Seychelles. One hundred sunkissed islands, as unique as they are beautiful. Soft, white coral sands that dip invitingly into crystal clear waters. Year-round sunshine that gives life to many unique plants and wildlife. These are the islands of your dreams—unique by a thousand miles. Reach for them today. Clip the coupon for your free colour brochure or see your travel agent.

Seychelles
Unique by a thousand miles

Text 4 shows three features typical of advertisements:

A cleverly worded headline
Out of this world, but not out of your reach.

A theme — in this example, it is isolation and uniqueness
A thousand miles from anywhere . . .
. . . as unique as they are beautiful.
. . . many unique plants and wildlife.

A memorable signature line linked to the theme
Unique by a thousand miles

Did your advertisement have some or all of these features?
If it didn't, try to change it so that it does.

Task 3

Advertising copy-writers make clever use of the resources of the
language. Parallelism and contrast are two features which are widely
used, e.g.
Out of this world,
but not out of your reach.
The same feature is used in this Volvo advertisement in which even
the lay-out of the first two sentences emphasizes the parallelism.

Text 5

From 0-60 in 8·5 seconds.
From showroom to scrapyard in
19·3 years.
    Government statistics in
Sweden show that the average
Volvo has a life expectancy of 19·3
years. (Longer than any other car
tested.)
    So although the 760 Turbo
may be the quickest production car
we've ever built (top speed 125
mph) in one respect, we expect it to
be slower than the competition.
    It will take ages to age.
    The Volvo 760 Turbo.

Text 5 also contains another language feature typical of advertising. Underline all of the comparatives and superlatives in the text.

- What is the theme (or central idea) of the advertisement?
- How do the comparatives and superlatives match the theme of the advertisement?
- How has the copy-writer played on the word 'age'? How does such wordplay emphasize the theme?
- What image of their product do Volvo project?

Task 4

Rewrite Text 5 so that the parallelism and comparison are removed. Begin like this:
The Volvo 760 Turbo can accelerate from 0–60mph in 8.5 seconds. It will also last for 19.3 years because . . .

Compare your rewrite with the original text. Which one is more interesting and memorable?

4   Doing your own thing

Task 1

Form two pairs. Each pair is to decide on a product or service which they want to advertise. They should also decide on the market they wish to reach and the image which they wish to promote.

Get together with the other pair, and tell them all about your product and commission them to write a display advertisement for you. They also tell you about their product, and commission you to write an advertisement for them.

You and your partner are now copy-writers. Write the copy, and then meet your clients (the other pair) and show them the advertisement. Discuss it with them and defend your choice of language and theme. If necessary, change both to improve your advertisement.

The following words may be useful. They include the adjectives and verbs most commonly used in television advertising.

adjectives

new	*good/better/best*	*free*
fresh	*delicious*	*wonderful*
special	*fine*	*great*
real	*extra*	*rich*

verbs

make	*go*	*feel*
get	*know*	*choose*
have	*keep*	*take*
see	*need*	*start*
look	*like*	*taste*
buy	*love*	*use*
	come	

Note that, with the exception of *use*, the verbs are all of Anglo-Saxon origin. In general, it is the Germanic vocabulary which is associated with colloquial, informal English of the style common in advertising.

You may also find it useful to refer to a thesaurus for vocabulary, and to examples of display advertisements in magazines for ideas. However, you shouldn't just copy another advertisement. The effectiveness of an advertisement depends on its being different from other advertisements.

5

Putting a point of view

1 Introduction

It is easy to be annoyed by things. It is less easy to write an article or letter about such annoyance in a way that will convince people that something could — or should — be done to alleviate or even remove the problem. Arousing the reader's interest, clearly outlining the problem and succinctly suggesting solutions requires skill in finding good ideas and organizing and expressing them effectively. It is with such matters that this unit will be concerned.

2 Showing what you think about something

Task 1

Have you ever been annoyed or inconvenienced by something?
Such as:

buses that don't travel on time
people making a noise late at night
inconsiderate car drivers
queueing in banks and shops
delays at the supermarket check-out.

With a partner, discuss some of the things which have annoyed or inconvenienced you. Exchange experiences and then make a list of the things which have inconvenienced or annoyed you.

Find another partner, and compare your list with your second partner's list. Ask each other why things were included on the list. Talk about incidents or occasions when you have been annoyed or inconvenienced.

Task 2

You have now got a lot of ideas on things which annoy people.
Probably some things which annoy other people don't annoy you.
Find out from a third partner if there are any things on your list which
don't annoy him/her. Ask why these things don't annoy your partner.
Give reasons why some of the things annoy you.

Task 3

Being annoyed or inconvenienced about something is one problem.
Doing something about the matter concerned is another. It is easy to
complain, but less easy to change things.

Take one of the things on your list. It should be something that you
really feel quite strongly about. Try to think of at least two ways in
which you could improve things so as to remove, or at least reduce,
the inconvenience or annoyance. For instance, if you are annoyed
about delays at the supermarket check-out, you could suggest
employing more staff or installing more efficient cash registers.

Discuss your suggestions with a partner. If you feel that your
partner's suggestions for improvements are not very realistic or are
not very sensible, tell your partner about your objections. Try to
think of ways of meeting your partner's objections.

Task 4

After the discussions you have had, you should now have the
following:

a topic, e.g. delays at the supermarket check-out
a thesis, e.g. supermarket shopping needs to be improved
examples of what happens
suggestions for improving or remedying things.

If we want to write about such a subject, there are at least two ways
of organizing the points to be covered.

1
- the thesis (i.e. what the problem is)
- examples of the problem from your own experience
- how you feel about the problem
- suggestions for overcoming the problem

2
- examples of the problem from your own experience
- the thesis (i.e. what the problem is)
- how you feel about the problem
- suggestions for overcoming the problem

With a partner, discuss other ways of organizing the above points.
Use your own examples and arrange and rearrange the points in
different ways. Which ways do you find to be best?

Task 5

Now that you have worked out a list of points and ways of organizing them, write a short composition on the topic or theme you have chosen. Organize your points in the most effective order, based on the work you did in Task 4.

When you have finished writing, exchange compositions with a partner and read his or hers. Discuss the compositions together. Tell your partner what you thought of his or her composition, and ask why it was organized in the way it was. Tell your partner why you organized your ideas in the way you did. Discuss ways in which you could have improved your composition.

3   Arguing and suggesting

Task 1

Now that you have written your own composition, putting your point of view on something, you may find it interesting to see how someone else did the same thing. The extract below is from a newspaper article by Giles Gordon called 'Slovenly queues'.
The paragraphs in the text are given in the wrong sequence. There is also a jumbled list of headings. There are five headings and four paragraphs. Work with a partner and match the headings with the paragraphs, then put the paragraphs into the correct order.

Headings

☐   Reasons
☐   Example
☐   The thesis or problem
☐   Suggested solution
☐   Example

Paragraphs

a   Likewise at railway stations, box offices, travel agencies, theatre bars, post offices and everywhere else where it is necessary to queue before being served and where there is more than one line.

b   Why can't we adopt the simple system that other countries do, but only a very few enlightened organisations here do? Namely, that when you enter your bank (or wherever), you join the end of the single queue or line there is, and the person at the head of the queue advances towards the first unoccupied cashier when the previous customer has departed; and thus until it is your turn. First come, first served.

c   If there are three queues in the bank, I invariably pick the one that moves most slowly. Those who arrive later than me and join queues which at the time are longer end up in front of the cashier before I do.

d The slovenly way in which we British organise — or rather do not organise — our queueing procedures irritates and frustrates for two reasons above all. First, it just isn't fair (and queueing is supposed to be about fairness) that he or she who has arrived second or third or fourth should be dealt with first. It offends against logic and the law-abiding members of the community. Second, it's a waste of time (and queueing is ostensibly to save time).

Task 2

Having put the paragraphs in the correct sequence, compare the way in which Mr Gordon organized his points with the way you organized yours.

- He began with two examples. Why is this quite an effective way to start such a composition?
- What is the effect if you put the thesis paragraph first?
- What expression does he use in order to introduce his suggested solution?
- What is the effect of using the following sentences to introduce the solution?

I suggest that we use the simple system . . .
It would be much better if we used the simple system . . .
I believe that we should use the simple system . . .
Using the simple system followed in other countries would be better.

Task 3

When stating his reasons for criticizing the queueing practices in Britain, Mr Gordon carefully listed them. Ring the two words he uses to list his reasons. Write out at least two other ways he could have used to list his two reasons.

Try your suggested alternatives with his sentences. What is the effect? What ways did you use for introducing the reasons in your own composition? Are some of the alternatives better?

Task 4

Mr Gordon goes on to give two other examples of bad queueing, and he provides a suggested solution to one of them. Then he ends his discussion with the following paragraphs. Which paragraph comes at the end of his article?

It shouldn't be beyond the powers of those in authority in organisations both large and small, public and private, to make standing in line less painful, more palatable.

The queueing principle brings out the worst in people, especially in cities. The naturally aggressive become more belligerent, the unnaturally timid more nervous. It is an embarrassment and humiliation to all but the most insensitive souls.

In the second of the two paragraphs above, Mr Gordon makes a general statement followed by a general example. His example is written as a sentence in two parallel halves:

The naturally aggressive become more belligerent,
the unnaturally timid more nervous.

Find the parallelism and contrast in the other paragraph.

Were there any statements in your own composition which could have been expressed by a similar type of parallelism and contrast? What is the effect of writing such a statement in this way?

Task 5

Take another topic about which you feel strongly. Write down as many ideas as you can on the topic and identify a thesis, i.e. the point or problem which you wish to write about.

Write a composition, organized in the best way you think for the topic and thesis concerned. Try to begin with an interesting or attention-getting opening, and end with a clearly stated solution.

If you wish, use some of the features that you studied in Tasks 2, 3 and 4.

Incidentally, Mr Gordon's complaint may have had some effect. The solution he suggests has been widely adopted in banks, post offices and other places where people queue for service.

1 Introduction

Writing publicly to express views on a current or proposed scheme involves developing an argument. This requires the writer to think of points for or against his or her viewpoint. In addition, it may require finding evidence in support of the points to be made.

The writer may try to persuade readers by appealing to logic or feeling or both. Appeals to common sense, to decency, honesty and propriety are appeals to feeling rather than logic. In the end, an emotional appeal may be more successful than a logical appeal, although a good writer will probably manage a balance between both kinds of appeal.

In this unit you will be asked to write a letter presenting an argument, and a second letter responding to the first. The letter will be written to the editor of a newspaper, so it is a public document, intended for a readership whose characteristics, knowledge and sympathies can only be guessed at.

2 Showing what you think about something

Task 1

Work in groups of three or four, and read Briefing sheet 1 (it is continued on page 44).

(it is continued on page 44).

Briefing sheet 1

Your role
Head teacher of a primary school

Age of pupils
5 to 11 years

School day
      08.45 to 12.00
lunch 12.00 to 13.00
      13.00 to 15.45

Travel to & from school
Most children walk, some with parents, others with other children. Some are driven to school by parents.
Over half the children go home for lunch.

Situation
The school is near a busy railway line carrying passenger and freight trains; there is a commuter service to the main city

Neighbourhood
Over half the children come from housing on the other side of the railway line from the school. There is a very popular park and recreation area on the same side of the railway line as the school.

6

Presenting and responding to an argument

Manually-controlled, full-width barriers

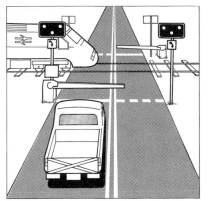

Automatically-controlled half-width barriers

Proposal by railway management
To replace the existing railway crossing gates. The present gates consist of a full width barrier which is controlled by a man. The new gates will each be half the width of the road, and they will be controlled automatically.

Extra information
In 1983, 430 automatic crossings were in use. Two people were killed in accidents at crossings. The installation of a full barrier controlled by closed-circuit TV would cost £80,000.

Discuss the likely effects of the proposal on your school.

Discuss arguments against the proposal and think of as many different arguments as you can. Your arguments can deal with:

safety
danger
convenience
inconvenience
cost
the people likely to be affected by the proposal.

Evaluate the arguments and put them into whatever seem to be the most appropriate groupings, e.g.

the stronger arguments
those that are logically sound
those that have an emotional appeal
those that deal with economic considerations
those that consider safety
etc.

Reject any arguments which don't seem to be sensible, sound or logical.

Task 2

Using the arguments you have agreed are best, write a letter to the editor of the local newspaper. In your letter, argue against the proposal and present the arguments you developed in Task 1 to support your case. Consider who is going to read your letter, how much the reader will know of the situation and how you can appeal to him or her.

Task 3

Exchange letters with another group. Read the other group's letter and discuss it together. Consider their arguments. Criticise them and suggest counter arguments. For each point that they make, you should be able to think of a counter argument. Organize your counter arguments as you did in Task 1.

Task 4

Read Briefing sheet 2.

Briefing sheet 2

Your role
An official of the railway company

Information
During the past 20 years, only two people have been killed or injured at automatic crossings.
There are strict guidelines for such installations.
The Railway Inspectorate advises the Department of Transport on such installations.
The proper procedures were followed before finalizing the proposal.

Using the other group's letter as a basis, discuss a reply to their letter which will include the counter arguments that you produced in Task 3 and a short but effective conclusion.

Write the letter and exchange it with the original group. Comment on each other's replies.

3   Writing to the editor

Task 1

Read the three texts on page 46.

- What is the attitude of each writer towards the subject of the argument?
- Which reply to Mrs Moore's letter is, in your view, more effective? Why?

Compare these letters with the ones you and your group wrote in the previous exercises. What features in these three texts could you use to improve your own letters?

Text 1

Level-crossing danger

From Councillor Mrs Ann Moore

Sir. The anxiety expressed by the staff and governors of Cherry Hinton Infants' School (June 27) about the dangers of automatic half-barriers at level crossings near schools, is fully shared by the people of Etchingham, in East Sussex.

British Rail is proposing to install these here, too — in our case in place of a skirted full barrier — in order to save the cost of having a manned signal box at Etchingham station. At present the barrier is operated by the signalman.

Etchingham Primary School is not adjacent to the crossing, but it is separated from the main village by the railway line, so that every child resident in the village itself has to use the crossing twice a day. They have to walk along a busy main road, much of which has no footway. This will mean that a child correctly walking facing the traffic will reach the crossing at the point where there is no barrier at all — the half of the "half-barrier" which is unguarded. Parents rightly feel this is unacceptably dangerous, even though they all accompany their children to and from the school.

There will be a further risk to unaccompanied children in the holidays. The crossing lies between the village and open country which offers the delights of fishing in the river and playing in the fields. Who can say that a child cyclist will never try to dodge through the barriers, or play "last across" for a dare?

Added to this, the Etchingham crossing is next to a busy commuter station. BR is to close the car park on the "up" side of the line, leaving only the one on the "down" side. Can one be sure that no commuter, delayed by traffic, will ever risk dodging through rather than miss his train? The recent tragic accident (report, June 22) suggests the answer to this question.

A full-skirted four-bar barrier could be installed at Etchingham and controlled by closed-circuit television from the neighbouring station of Robertsbridge, we are told, at a cost of about £80,000. We are also told this would be "too expensive". Surely even one human life is worth that?
Yours faithfully,
ANN MOORE,
Hancox,
Whatlington,
Battle, East Sussex.
July 1.

Text 2

Level-crossing safety

From Mr G. C. Pettitt

Sir. The risks to the safety of children which Councillor Moore (July 5) believes will exist at Etchingham when automatic half-barriers are installed are not supported by experience. There are now 280 automatic half-barrier crossings in operation on British Rail and since the first types were installed over 20 years ago no child pedestrian has been killed or even injured by a train at an automatic crossing.

The guidelines governing the design and installation of level-crossing equipment are strict. Every application requires the personal examination of a Department of Transport railway inspector who will satisfy himself that the plans meet the guidelines and always visits the proposed location.

Final approval is only given by the Secretary of State after full consultation with the Railway Inspectorate and the highway and local authority involved. The proposal to install automatic crossing equipment at Etchingham has been subjected to this rigorous procedure.

Councillor Moore also says that there will be increased danger to pedestrians when the up-side car park is closed. She can be reassured on this point as we now have no plans to close it.
Yours faithfully,
GORDON PETTITT,
General Manager,
British Rail, Waterloo Station, SE1.

Text 3

From the Editor of Railway Gazette International

Sir. Back in 1968, a Southern Region official assured me that "we shall close the line from Tonbridge to Hastings within 10 years". Now it is being electrified and resignalled at a cost of £24m, which means that communities like Battle and Etchingham will not only keep their trains but enjoy a better service.

How depressing, therefore, to read in your columns (June 27 and July 5) ill-informed criticism of automatic level crossings being installed under this scheme. The independent Oppenheim report found in 1983 that all types of automatic level crossing were safe for pedestrians. In that year there were just two deaths at 403 automatic crossings, only one being an (elderly) pedestrian.

The widespread belief that schoolchildren are at risk on automatic level crossings is nonsense; whereas reckless motorists do sometimes ignore the red lights — and pay the penalty, as at road junctions — I cannot recall a single case of children being killed in this way.

The real threat to Etchingham's children is from road traffic, which kills 2,000 pedestrians every year with scarcely a murmur of public protest.
Yours faithfully,
RICHARD HOPE, Editor,
Railway Gazette International
Quadrant House,
Sutton,
Surrey.
July 5.

Task 2

Read Text 1 again and study how Mrs Moore organized her letter.

Write the number of each paragraph next to the appropriate function. (Two paragraphs have the same function.) The functions are listed below in random order.

Para no.	Function
	Providing further evidence against the decision
	Making an alternative suggestion
	Describing the current situation and predicting the outcome of the recent decision
	Reporting on a recent decision
	Informing the reader of the topic of the letter

Clear presentation of an argument involves signalling the force and arrangement of ideas to the reader. Mrs Moore uses two types of signals:

logical signals to show contrast or consequence
attitudinal signals to show her attitude or feelings.

Attitudinal signals are often *-ly* adverbs, such as

actually
really
admittedly
certainly

as well as such phrases as

in (actual) fact
in reality
of course.

Reread Mrs Moore's letter and put the appropriate signals from her letter in the blank spaces below.

X is not A, ... it is B, ... C is a consequence.
Y happens. . . . . Z will follow.
People . . . . believe that Z is D,
. . . . people take care to avoid D.

Find the other attitudinal signal in the final paragraph of Mrs Moore's letter and together with the signals you wrote in the passage above, add it to the list given above.

Refer back to your own letter. What signals did you use? Can you improve your letter by adding appropriate signals, reorganizing your ideas and signalling them more clearly?

Task 3

Mrs Moore also makes use of another technique to add force to her argument:

Who can say that a child cyclist will never try to dodge through the barriers, or play 'last across' for a dare?

Mrs Moore's rhetorical question anticipates the answer 'No one'. In other words, no one can really claim that children will never take risks at such a crossing. Therefore, so Mrs Moore's argument runs, such barriers are unsafe because there is always the possibility that a child may take a risk and be killed as a consequence.

Find the other two examples of this use of rhetorical questions in her letter, and copy them out.

What answers do Mrs Moore's questions anticipate? How do her questions contribute to her argument?

Mrs Moore's final question tells the reader quite a lot about her attitude to the subject. What is her attitude? What attitude would be expressed by a negative answer to her question? Would this be a socially acceptable attitude?

Task 4

Mrs Moore uses the passive voice several times. Rewrite these sentences in the active voice:

The anxiety . . . is shared by the people of Etchingham.
A full-skirted four-bar barrier could be installed at Etchingham and controlled by closed-circuit television . . . , we are told . . .
We are also told this would be . . .

Is the active voice version any better? Is it as appropriate to the purpose and tone of the letter?

Review your own letters and see if there are any statements which would be better rewritten in the passive voice if they are active, or in the active voice if they are passive.

Underline all the examples of the passive voice in Mr Pettit's letter (Text 2). Rewrite them in the active voice. What is the effect now? Is it the effect that Mr Pettit would intend? Why does Mr Pettit use the passive voice as he does?

Task 5

When presenting or responding to an argument, it is usually important to give evidence in support of the arguments which are being put forward.

In Mrs Moore's letter, the evidence was presented in her description of the situation of the school, the village and the countryside in relation to the railway crossing. In Mr Pettit's letter, he gave two sorts of objective evidence:
statistical — 280 barriers, 20 years, no deaths
procedural — steps taken before installing an automatic crossing.

Read Mr Hope's letter and underline the evidence he gives in favour of automatic crossings. Classify his evidence under the two headings below.

Objective	*Subjective*

What is the problem with subjective evidence in an argument? Read your own letters. Is there any subjective evidence in them? Can you substitute objective evidence for it?

Task 6

Rewrite your letters, incorporating any improvements that have been developed as a result of studying the three letters.

4   Responding to an argument

Task 1

Either
Write letters in the roles given in Briefing sheets 3 and 4 on pages 50 and 51. As in the earlier exercises, your letters are to appear in the Letters to the Editor section of a newspaper. Follow the same discussing, planning, drafting and writing procedures as you did earlier in this unit.

or
Write about an issue of importance to you or members of your class. Discuss the issue first and write down arguments on separate pieces of paper. Write down any evidence you can use to support your arguments. Arrange the arguments into the best order. This can

easily be done by arranging and rearranging your sheets of paper.
Think of a good opening and concluding statement.

Exchange letters with another group, and write a reply to their
letter. Follow similar procedures to those you followed when writing
your own letter.

Briefing sheet 3

Your role
Head teacher of a primary school

Age of pupils
5 to 11 years

School day
      08.45 to 12.00
lunch 12.00 to 13.00
      13.00 to 15.45

Travel to & from school
Most children walk, some with parents, others with other
children. Some are driven to school by parents.
Over half the children go home for lunch.

Situation
The school is on a quiet suburban street. Nearby there is a link
road to the motorway. The area in which the school is situated is
between the motorway and an industrial area.

Neighbourhood
Residential, mostly with younger families with children. There is a
shopping centre opposite the school.

Proposal
To link the street in which the school is situated to the nearby
motorway link by installing a roundabout.

Result
The school street will become the shortest route between the
motorway and the industrial area.

Extra information
2,000 pedestrians a year die in road traffic accidents.
The new roundabout will cost £50,000.
A new ring road would cost £850,000.

Briefing sheet 4

Your role
An official of the local authority Road Planning Department.

Information
The Department of Transport advises on such road developments.
They have given their approval.
Heavy traffic will not be allowed to use the suburban road.
There will be traffic lights to control a new pedestrian crossing
from the school to the shopping centre.

Developing a theme

1 Introduction

One of the things which characterizes effective writing is the way in which a writer identifies and sustains a theme. The theme is the idea which dominates and helps to give shape and movement to a piece of writing. A theme tells the reader what to expect, and by providing a framework or a main idea, it helps the reader to make sense of the rest of what he or she reads.

In this unit, you will write an essay on a given theme. You will do this in a number of stages, each of which is designed to help you:

identify a theme
develop it
organize ideas around the theme
express the ideas effectively.

The activities which you will do should help you to generate ideas when, on being given a writing task, your mind goes blank.

2 Establishing and developing a theme

Task 1

In some types of writing, a theme is very clearly introduced and developed. Advertising copy-writers and journalists very commonly use a clearly stated theme as a focus.

Read Texts 1 and 2 (opposite) and state in one short sentence what the theme of each text is.

Text 1

'To travel hopefully is a better thing than to arrive and the true success is to labour,' wrote Robert Louis Stevenson in his essay *El Dorado*. A week's holiday in Suffolk by local buses has almost converted me to his view.

'*Moving Picture of Constable Country*' Jean Sargeant

Text 2

Could this be the quietest car launch ever?

When we designed the new Toyota Camry we took a vow of silence.

We started with a passenger compartment, lined throughout with soundproofing. No less than 3 layers are used in the most critical areas.

To cut wind noise to a bare whisper, flush fitting glass was the order of the day.

We developed a suspension system that actually suppresses road noise.

(What it does to bumps and potholes is another advertisement altogether.)

Finally, we endowed the Camry with a 16 valve engine that is the epitome of smoothness.

(Quiet it may be. Our new car still manages to outpace every one of its 2 litre rivals.)

The result is a car that's as tranquil as a Trappist's cell. Though hardly as Spartan.

In fact, you might accuse us of pandering to the materialist.

In both its saloon and estate forms, the GLi is blessed with electric windows, central locking and a refined stereo system.

Even the aerial is electrically operated.

In addition, the GLi Executive comes with cruise control, air conditioning and an electric sunroof.

We could go on. Instead, may we recommend a visit to your Toyota showroom. The new Camry is decidedly a car to be seen.

And not heard.

TOYOTA
THE NEW CAMRY

Once a writer has decided on a theme, other ideas follow. Although the ideas may not come easily, they will come a lot more easily than if the writer has no central idea to develop.

In Text 2 the central idea of silence establishes a unifying theme which not only emphasizes the advertiser's message — it also adds to the readability and memorability of the copy.

Read Text 2 again and identify all the words and phrases associated with silence.

Complete the sentences below:

The new Camry is decidedly a car to be . . . .

And not . . . .

These final sentences of the copy round off the advertisement very effectively, reminding the reader of both the theme and the qualities of the product.

Task 2

Advertising and journalism are not the only types of writing in which establishing and developing a theme is important. Here are two paragraphs from very different sources. The first is from a book written by an educationist — Jerome Bruner — while the second is from an essay by George Orwell.

Read the paragraphs and state the theme of each in one word or phrase. Discuss how you think each passage will continue.

Text 3

The single most characteristic thing about human beings is that they learn. Learning is so deeply ingrained in man that it is almost involuntary, and thoughtful students of human behavior have even speculated that our specialization as a species is a specialization for learning. For, by comparison with organisms lower in the animal kingdom, we are ill equipped with prepared reflex mechanisms. As William James put it decades ago, even our instinctive behavior occurs only once, thereafter being modified by experience. With a half century's perspective on the discoveries of Pavlov, we know that man not only is conditioned by his environment, but may be so conditioned even against his will.

Toward a Theory of Instruction Jerome S. Bruner

Text 4

National characteristics are not easy to pin down, and when pinned down they often turn out to be trivialities or seem to have no connection with one another. Spaniards are cruel to animals, Italians can do nothing without making a deafening noise, the Chinese are addicted to gambling. Obviously such things don't matter in themselves. Nevertheless, nothing is causeless, and even the fact that Englishmen have bad teeth can tell one something about the realities of English life.

'England Your England' in *Inside the Whale and Other Essays*
George Orwell

Read the sentences below which could open the next paragraph in Texts 3 and 4. In each case, only one sentence is from the original. Which sentence to you think is likely to be the one actually written by the author? Why? Discuss your ideas with a partner.

Bruner
Curiosity is an instinctive motive in human beings.
Why then invoke the idea of a 'will to learn'?
Coping with the environment is developed by practice.

Orwell
When one returns to England after a period abroad, one has the sensation of breathing a different air.
Yet England, together with the rest of the world, is changing.
Here are a couple of generalizations about England that would be accepted by almost all observers.

Task 3

When you are trying to produce ideas for a theme, you can use the following idea-generating processes:

A Associate the theme with something else.
D Define it.
A Apply the idea.
D Describe it.
C Compare it with something else.
A Argue for or against the subject.
N Narrate the development or history of it.

This yields the mnemonic:

A DAD CAN

You can use this mnemonic to recall idea-generating processes when you are trying to produce ideas for a writing assignment.

Below are a number of themes. Classify them into two types — general and specific.

A journey by air

Food

Travel

Traditional arts and crafts in my country

The environmental effects of acid rain

The problems of being a foreigner in a strange country

Pets

Problems

A description of your town for visitors

Overcoming examination nerves

The environment

Education for leisure and unemployment

Success

Famine, hunger and the provision of international relief

My favourite sport or game

Changing patterns of child rearing in modern society

Computers

Friendship

Choose one general theme and one specific theme. Use the idea-generating processes to develop each theme. Discuss your ideas with a partner and decide which ideas would be the best as the basis for an essay.

As you may have discovered, a general theme gives you plenty of opportunity to develop the theme as you wish. This can be an advantage if you have a lot of ideas. If, however, you have only a few ideas, a general theme can cause difficulties. In that case, a specific theme can be more helpful, as it provides you with a guide to a way of developing the theme. If you are working under time pressure, as in an examination, you may be wise to choose a specific theme when writing an essay. If, however, you prefer to develop an essay in your own way, and if you can produce ideas quickly, a general theme may suit you better.

Task 4

In Task 2 you read the opening paragraph of a chapter in Jerome S. Bruner's book, *Toward a Theory of Instruction.* In the next paragraph, Bruner states his theme in the opening sentence, which is given as a question:

Why then invoke the idea of a 'will to learn'?

Bruner's theme, 'The will to learn', is the theme you are going to write about in this unit. Write down quickly all the ideas which this theme gives rise to. (If you get stuck, use the mnemonic A DAD CAN to help stimulate ideas.)

Discuss your ideas and compare them with those of a partner. Use your partner's ideas to stimulate more of your own. Write them down.

Task 5

The first stage in writing is producing ideas. The next is to develop these ideas from a random assortment into an organized theme. There are at least two possibilities:

Method 1
Sort the ideas you have written down into different groups so that you can begin to see some pattern or significance in the ideas.

Method 2
Take any one of the ideas that you have produced, and use the 'nutshelling' technique to identify a theme. To do this:

- Write as much as you can as quickly as possible.
- After writing about 6 or 8 lines, read over what you have written.
- What is the main idea in what you have written so far?
- Write a summary sentence which states the main idea — in other words summarize the ideas 'in a nutshell'.
- Use the 'nutshell' statement to begin another sequence of sentences.
- Nutshell again, and repeat the procedure once again if you wish.

By now, what you write as your summary of the main idea should be your theme. If you're still stuck, discuss your ideas with a partner. You may be able to identify each other's themes more easily than your own.

The 'nutshelling' process can help you to discover the idea or theme that you want to develop, even when you have already been given a general theme to write about, such as 'The will to learn'.

Return to 'The will to learn' (Task 4).

Step A

Read through your notes and organize the ideas to show a pattern. Take one of the main ideas and begin writing. 'Nutshell' what you have written. Repeat this process once or twice.

Step B

Discuss with a partner what you have done and the central idea that has emerged during the nutshelling process. Compare and contrast your approaches, your ideas and what you have written. Discuss how you think your ideas will develop.

Task 6

By now you should have developed a general plan for the theme 'The will to learn'. Either you will have the plan in your head, or you will have written it in your notes.

So far, you have worked on the theme without considering who you are going to write for, i.e. who your reader is, and why you are writing, i.e. what your purpose is.

If you are writing an essay in an examination, the reader is the examiner. An examiner is a rather peculiar type of reader, since he or she reads in order to judge or assess, unlike most readers who read in order to be:

entertained
informed
instructed
persuaded
reinforced in existing relationships.

Unless you have a specific audience in mind, it helps to think of your reader for an examination or classwork assignment as being a mixture of someone like yourself and someone like your teacher.

This means that in developing your theme, you should ask such questions as:

- Why would I want to read about it?
- What do I already know about it?
- What would I want to learn about it?

Keeping these questions in mind, review your ideas on the theme 'The will to learn' and add or delete ideas. Discuss what you have done with a partner and compare and contrast what you have written. Discuss what you think your reader will want to learn when reading your essay.

3   Organizing ideas

Task 1

Producing and organizing ideas is one thing. Shaping ideas and the organization of your writing for a reader is another. But often the most difficult part of writing can be starting a first draft. Fortunately, there are a number of ways in which you can begin an essay. In each case, the way you begin should be relevant to your theme. Here are some ways of opening an essay on 'Fear'.

Method	Example
Fact	Fear is a response to a threat which can be measured physiologically.
Opinion	Fear of failing is a burden which many of us carry around, like an unwanted burden, from which death itself may seem the only means of escape.
Event	As the 'thwack, thwack, thwack' sound of helicopters approached, the villagers ran for cover. While some people snatched their little children, others seized their rifles.
Speech	'This is the captain speaking,' said a voice over the intercom. 'We have a slight problem. All four engines have stopped.'
Anecdote	Once I was travelling at high speed along the Delta Highway between Alexandria and Cairo. Suddenly, in front of us, two trucks collided, spilling oil and grain all over the road. It happened as if in slow motion, and before one had time to reflect on it. Fortunately, our driver avoided a collision, and it was only afterwards that we began to feel afraid — afraid of what might have happened.
Quotation	'No passion so effectively robs the mind of all its powers of acting and reasoning as fear.' So wrote Edmund Burke in the eighteenth century.

The opening should engage the reader's interest and give a hint of what is to follow.

Generally, as readers, we prefer to be given an overview of the theme first. When the aim is to develop a sense of suspense, as in an anecdote (Unit 3) or a short story (Unit 12), the writer will hold information back, gradually revealing it piece by piece. In an essay whose function is to inform, instruct or persuade, it is usually better to begin with an overview. If, however, the function is to entertain, it may be better to create a sense of suspense.

Return to your theme, 'The will to learn', and begin to write your essay, following the most appropriate method for the ideas which you wish to develop. Exchange openings with a partner, and compare them.

Task 2

It can help to see how other writers begin. There are some examples earlier in this unit and there are some others below.

Read these openings and discuss the methods used. Say what the theme is in each case and consider how it will be developed. Decide which beginnings appeal to you and why they do.

Improve the opening to your own essay if you can, by following the method of one of these examples.

Example 1
'Since 'tis Nature's Law to change
Constancy alone is strange.'
John Wilmot, Earl of Rochester

A Dialogue between Strephon and Daphne
Everything in this universe is perpetually in a stage of change, a fact commented on by philosphers and poets through the ages. If we flick through any book of quotations we find numerous statements about the fluctuating world we live in: 'Everything rolls on, nothing stays still', claimed the ancient Greek philosopher Heraclitus in the sixth century BC. In the sixteenth century, Edmund Spenser speaks of 'the ever-whirling wheel of change, the which all mortal things doth sway', while 'time and the world are ever in flight' is a statement by the twentieth century Irish poet William Butler Yeats — to take just a few random samples.
    Language, like everything else, joins in this general flux . . .

Language Change: Progress or Decay? Jean Aitchison

Example 2
A society is a group of unequal beings organized to meet common needs.

In any sexually reproducing species, equality of individuals is a natural impossibility. Inequality must therefore be regarded as the first law of social materials, whether in human or other societies. Equality of opportunity must be regarded among vertebrate species as the second law . . .

The Social Contract Robert Ardrey

Example 3
Most journeys begin less abruptly than they end, and to fix the true beginning of this one in either time or space is a task which I do not care to undertake. I find it easier to open my account of it at the moment when I first realized, with a small shock of pleasure and surprise, that it had actually begun.

News From Tartary Peter Fleming

Example 4

As I write, highly civilized human beings are flying overhead, trying to kill me.

    They do not feel any enmity against me as an individual nor I against them. They are 'only doing their duty', as the saying goes. Most of them, I have no doubt, are kind-hearted law-abiding men who would never dream of committing murder in private life. On the other hand, if one of them succeeds in blowing me to pieces with a well-placed bomb, he will never sleep any the worse for it. He is serving his country, which has the power to absolve him from evil.

'England Your England' in *Inside the Whale and Other Essays*
George Orwell

Example 5

The food we eat is the main single cause of the diseases from which most of us eventually suffer and die. To be blunt, western food is a killer. The food we eat greatly increases our chances of suffering and dying from heart disease, stroke, and cancers — the three illnesses which jointly kill two out of every three people in Britain.

'The Food Scandal' *The Times*, Geoffrey Cannon

Task 3

So far, we have worked on:

producing ideas
organizing ideas
developing a theme
evolving a plan
taking account of your audience
getting started.

As you write, your ideas will continue to evolve, even though you will have an overall plan to guide you. And as you write, you will move from one step in your narrative, or one stage in your argument, to the next. To help both yourself and your reader, you will have to break up your text into paragraphs.

Paragraphs serve two functions — they break up a long piece of text into smaller visual units and they tell the reader to expect a new idea. In general, one paragraph = one main idea/one main stage. You may not get your paragraph organization right when writing your first draft. When you review your first draft, you should change paragraph boundaries if necessary. You may also find that you need to add or delete sentences so as to improve the continuity or flow from one paragraph to another.

Below there are some endings and beginnings of consecutive paragraphs. They have been run together so that the paragraph boundaries have been lost. Read these paragraph segments and discuss where the writer probably begins a new paragraph. Discuss how a connection is made between the two paragraphs. This may be through backward or forward pointing reference, e.g.

The man . . .
As we have seen . . .
Now we shall turn to . . .

or through the further development of an idea or action begun in the preceding paragraph, e.g.

However, . . .   Some time later . . .
In contrast to . . .   Compared with . . .

Example 1
. . . As soon as I saw the dead man I sent an orderly to a friend's house nearby to borrow an elephant rifle. I had already sent back the pony, not wanting it to go mad with fright and throw me if it smelt the elephant. The orderly came back in a few minutes with a rifle and five cartridges, and meanwhile some Burmans had arrived and told us that the elephant was in the paddy fields below, only a few hundred yards away . . .

'Shooting an Elephant' George Orwell

Example 2
. . . We simply note that the grammatical rules of a language are likely to alter slightly from region to region, and we then try to specify what these alterations are — though we must not expect abrupt changes between areas, more a gradual shifting with no clear-cut breaks. Parallel to geographical variation, we find social variation . . .

Language Change: Progress or Decay? Jean Aitchison

Example 3
. . . Their huts were as primitive as they could well have been: shelters made of branches and just big enough for four or five people at the most to huddle in at night. One end of the hut was kept open, and here a fire usually smouldered to keep the mosquitoes at bay, though whether or not a mosquito could have bitten through all that dirt and pipeclay it was difficult to say. Fire they made by taking a pointed stick and twirling it rapidly round with the palms of their hands on a base of soft wood, a thing they could do in the space of two minutes . . .

The Fatal Impact Alan Moorehead

Example 4
. . . if it came to fighting a court case, the dealer and perhaps manufacturer would no doubt field a formidable force of technical witnesses to show that they'd done everything possible to fix things — and that really a replacement car wasn't part of the deal at all. However, makers say that they look at any claim under guarantee for a replacement car on its merits. A friendly approach to the dealer is probably best . . .

Which? Way to Run Your Car

Example 5
. . . When success comes, it takes the form of recognition that beyond
the few things we know there lies a domain of inference: that putting
together the two and two that we have yields astonishing results. But this
raises the issue of competence, to which we must turn next. For curiosity
is only one of the intrinsic motives for learning. The drive to achieve
competence is another . . .

Toward a Theory of Instruction Jerome S. Bruner

Task 4

Complete your first draft of 'The will to learn'.

Review the way you have organized and developed your ideas. Pay
particular attention to the order and grouping of ideas, to paragraph
boundaries, and to the connection of ideas between paragraphs.

Task 5

Ending a piece of writing is almost as difficult as beginning.
Fortunately, the beginning can provide a basis for the ending. This
was effectively demonstrated in Text 1, in which the opening and
closing sentences echo each other:

When we designed the new Toyota Camry we took a vow of silence.

The new Camry is decidedly a car to be seen.
And not heard.

Read the endings below. How has the writer, in each case,
concluded? Has the ending been by:

summing up
recommending
looking to the future
finishing the narrative?

Try to match some of these concluding paragraphs with the
paragraphs given in earlier tasks.

Example 1
In a word, then, coping and defending are not, in my opinion, processes
of the same kind that differ merely in degree. They differ in kind. What
poses the eternal challenge to the teacher is the knowledge that the
metaphoric processes can, when put under the constraints of conscious
problem solving, serve the interests of health functioning. Without those
constraints, they result in the crippling decline that comes from a
specialization on defense.

Example 2
Laker has gone, but his legacy must not be allowed to die. He may have
been a buccaneer and a corner-cutter, but in hidebound and restrictive
conditions, it is usually that type of person who innovates. A far greater

tragedy than Laker's spectacular crash will occur if governments allow the bad old days of IATA cartels and inter-airline price fixing to bring to an end, or at least impede, the progress of cheap air travel. The fact that Sir Freddie over-reached himself, and that the banks and others failed to bring him back on course on time, must not mean that his ideas and initiative disappear in the smoke and debris of Laker Airways.

Example 3
In brief, brain-damaged patients are suffering from a variety of muscular, neuromuscular and mental disorders, all of which impair the normal orderliness and efficiency of speech. Language change, on the other hand, occurs when people whose brains and muscles are acting normally speak fast and efficiently. It would be most surprising if there were any substantial links between the two.

Example 4
'That's that,' said Kini; and sighed. The journey was over.

Each will be appropriate, depending on what has come before. Check your own ending paragraph. Discuss it and compare it with that of a partner. Suggest ways of improving the endings and incorporate improvements in your draft.

Task 6

When you have written a first draft and reviewed it for ideas, organization, shape and development, you can focus on expression. This means looking at sentence structure, tense usage and vocabulary.

It is important to write clearly and economically. This can mean either rephrasing ideas in two sentence instead of one, or rewriting two longer sentences as one shorter sentence.

Tense usage is important, especially to show:

sequence of events in a narrative
the general versus the particular
whether an action or outcome is complete or still continuing.

Vocabulary is important to give precision of meaning, and to create an effect or develop a theme. Developing a theme through the use of related vocabulary was demonstrated in Text 1, and is studied in the next unit, 'A sense of place'.

Go over your first draft, looking for ways of improving sentence structure, tense usage and vocabulary.

Incorporate any changes in a final draft and either exchange final drafts with a partner, and read and evaluate each other's work, or give your final draft to your teacher for marking.

8

A sense of place

Temple of Apollo at Bassae, Greece, 18 March, 1849 Edward Lear
(Ashmolean Museum, Oxford)

1 Introduction

Both fiction and travel writers show an ability to create a sense of
place. In fiction the setting may form an important role in establishing
both a location and a feeling or atmosphere for action and character.
In travel writing, the reader will anticipate that the writer will create
a feeling of 'what it was like to be there'.

In both cases, the writers make use of detail. A sense of
verisimilitude and actuality is created by including details of things,
events, feelings. Such details are the result of observation: the good
writer observes carefully and may even make notes for subsequent
use.

2 Observing and noting

Task 1

Here are some notes which Gavin Young subsequently included in his
Slow Boats to China.

Text 1

A long, low line of trees and houses. Fishing boats bobbing around us
everywhere; we almost run one or two down, and the captain shouts at
the fishermen angrily. A lighthouse ashore, blue and white striped like a
barber's pole.

   Beaches ahead backed by palms, a patchwork of red roofs, more sails,
Arab style, very white. Many church spires.

   The last meal — tuna, cabbage, eggs, rice — is served by the little
cooks; I can't complain about the quantity or quality of food on the
Herman Mary.

Now the great sails are down, the bamboo booms — their 'bark' an inch thick — stowed, the huge mainsail lowered by means of a hand-turned iron winch. Suddenly the *Herman Mary* has a bare, plucked-chicken look; it is a hulk with two masts, a moth without wings.

At what point in this particular voyage do you think Young made these notes — the beginning, the middle or the end?

With a partner, go through the notes and classify what he describes under these headings:

Setting	
Things	
Events	
People	
Feelings	

Task 2

With a partner, rewrite Young's notes as a complete piece of description.
To do this, you will probably need to
• decide on a viewpoint that you wish to develop
• add verbs to some sentences
• change the tense from present to past (although you may prefer to retain the present tense)

- change the order of some items
- provide an introductory sentence or two to make clear that this is the end of a voyage
- write a concluding sentence or two to bring the ship safely to the wharf.

Compare your completed version with that written by another pair. Discuss any similarities or differences. Why did you write the completed version in the way you did? In particular, if you retained the present tense, you should be able to explain why you did so, and you should compare present and past tense versions.

Task 3

It may be easy to write interestingly on something like the end of a voyage by a sailing ship: many things happen, scenes change. It may be less easy to write about a static scene, such as the room you are sitting in at the moment. And yet an imaginative writer can create an interesting description from limited means — it all depends on observation and imagination.

By yourself, make a list of as many things as you can that you can see in the room you are sitting in. With a partner, compare your lists and discuss differences. Why, for instance, did you include certain things in your list, whereas your partner included other things?

Task 4

Your lists form the basis of a description. To convert the bare lists into an interesting piece of writing, you need to ask some questions:

- What viewpoint of the room shall I take: my own, or someone else's?
- What theme or idea can I use as a focus for describing the room?

For instance, you could describe the part that the room plays in your life (or that of your class); or you could give a factual description of the room; or you could describe your attitude towards the room — what and how you feel about it.

- What elements in my list match the viewpoint and theme I have chosen?
- How should I begin my description? You could start with:
  action
  a factual statement
  a short piece of dialogue
  a quotation or proverb relevant to your theme.

Finally, you should think about who you are writing the description for. Who, in other words, is your intended reader? What will your reader know about your subject? How do you wish to affect your reader? Do you wish, for instance, merely to inform the reader, or do you wish to share with him or her your own attitudes to and feelings upon the subject?

Write a paragraph describing the room you are sitting in, using your notes and the questions above. Exchange descriptions with a partner, and read and discuss each other's paragraphs.

Task 5

Text 2 is a description of an office which Gavin Young visited in Colombo in order to try to arrange a passage on a boat.

Text 2

Mr Missier's office was in a small rectangular loft at the top of steep wooden steps. You approached it from the street through a long shadowy room at the entrance of which clerks with the Hindu spot on their foreheads tabulated the weighing of sacks of small onions, potatoes, green and red chillies, dried prawns and peanuts. Sacks of these commodities were stacked against the walls. In an aroma of onions an old woman squatted in a corner chewing betel and squirts of betel juice marked the floor.

As my head slowly rose above the level of the office floor where Mr Missier made his living, I registered two pairs of legs, two waists and finally two pairs of hands stretched out to help me up the last three steps. An elderly voice said, 'Hullo, sir. Well, well . . .'

Mr Missier was sitting at a desk, looking at me over his spectacles. An elderly man with a long, thin face and nose, he stretched forward a bony hand. 'Please be seated.' . . .

The basic contents of Mr Missier's headquarters were whitewashed walls, a single overhead fan, two wall calendars, a tiny safe, a filing cabinet, three tables and six people, one of them a teaboy. There were other objects, of course: his desk, covered in black leatherette with a ziggurat of torn files; an umbrella hanging from the top of the plastic curtain over the bottom half of a window with rusty bars. The window opened outwards, and a large crow perched on the frame, cawing loudly. One of the clerks poked at it every now and then with the umbrella, and it flew off, returning a moment later to continue its cawing.

This is an extract from a much longer work than your description written in Task 4. However, you may find it useful to compare your description with Gavin Young's.

- What is the viewpoint which he adopts?
- What is the feeling which you, as a reader, obtain from his description?
- How important is detail in establishing a sense of place?
- What details strike you as being interesting or unusual?

Much description has a highly visual quality, and is organized like a series of shots in a film. With a partner, make a list of the shots that you would need in a film of this event in Gavin Young's story. Make a similar list of film shots for your own descriptive paragraph. Are there any features of your own description which could be improved by adopting a more pictorial approach, as in Young's account?

Task 6

Young uses uncomplicated sentence structure to create a picture of Mr Missier's office:

subject	**verb**	**adverbial complement**	
Mr Missier's office	*was*	*in a small rectangular loft . . .*	

subject	**verb**	**object**	**adverbial**
You	*approached*	*it*	*from the street . . .*

adverbial	**subject**	**verb**	**adverbial**
In an aroma of onions	*an old woman*	*squatted*	*in a corner . . .*

subject	**verb**	**complement**
The basic contents of Mr M's headquarters	*were*	*whitewashed walls . . .*

there	**verb**	**complement**
There	*were*	*other objects . . .*

Where the complexity comes is in the adverbial elements:

. . . in a small rectangular loft at the top of steep wooden steps
. . . from the street through a long shadowy room at the entrance of which clerks with the Hindu spot on their foreheads tabulated the weighing of sacks of small onions . . .

And in the complements:

whitewashed walls, a single overhead fan, two wall calendars . . .

It is in these two elements that Young provides the detailed information which makes the description so pictorial and vivid.

Underline all the other items included in the adverbial elements and complements in Young's description. Compare his use of such items with those in your own description. Could you have improved your own version by making greater use of more densely-packed adverbials and complements?

Rewrite some of your description, using more fully-packed adverbial and complement items. You may find that you have to include more information (which means that you will have to be more observant) or that you will need to reorganize your description.

Task 7

So far, we have been indoors, the focus of description being a room. Now it is time to move outdoors.

Write a description of a busy street. Your description is to convey an impression of the activity and noise of such a street. You will probably find it easier to work if you imagine a busy street that you have been in. Use your senses to make a list of things you saw, heard, smelt and felt.

When you have made such a list, decide on your viewpoint and theme.

The viewpoint can be literally the view of the street that you take, e.g. from the ground, from above, from a vehicle, etc. It can be your own viewpoint or someone else's. And it can involve the attitude that you adopt to the street — do you like it? Do you dislike it?

The theme will be the main idea that you wish to develop in your description. A busy street is more than just a busy street — it can be a symbol for something. If so, what? What does it symbolize for you? The symbol can be your theme.

Once you have chosen your viewpoint and theme, you can begin to draft your description, choosing elements from your list which will exemplify or develop your theme.

If you can't immediately think of a theme, begin writing anyway and use the 'nutshelling' process described in Unit 7 (page 56).

Task 8

In Text 3 Mary McCarthy describes a Florentine street. She begins the paragraph as follows:

Text 3

A 'characteristic' Florentine street — that is, a street which contains points of touristic interest (old palaces, a Michelozzo portal, the room where Dostoevsky finished *The Idiot*, etcetera) — is not only extremely narrow, poor, and heavily populated, lined with florists and greengrocers who display their wares on the strip of sidewalk, but it is also likely to be one of the principal traffic arteries.

After describing briefly the route and changes in name followed by the Via Romana, she then continues with the following passage.

- What is McCarthy's attitude to her subject?
- What is the theme (or main idea) which she develops in this passage?

The traffic on Via Romana is highly 'characteristic'. Along the narrow sidewalk, single file, walks a party of Swiss or German tourists, barelegged, with cameras and other equipment hanging bandoleer-style from various leather straps on their persons; clinging to the buildings, in their cleated shoes, they give the effect of a scaling party in the Alps. They are the only walkers, however, who are not in danger of death. Past them flows a confused stream of human beings and vehicles: baby carriages wheeling in and out of the Boboli Garden, old women hobbling in and out of church, grocery carts, bicycles, Vespas, Lambrettas, motorcycles, *topolinos*, Fiat *seicento*s, a trailer, a donkey cart from the country delivering sacks of laundry that has been washed with ashes, in the old-fashioned way, Cadillacs, Alfa-Romeos, *millecento*s, Chevrolets, a Jaguar, a Rolls-Royce with a chauffeur and a Florence licence plate, bands of brawny workmen carrying bureaus, mirrors, and credenzas (for this is the neighbourhood of the artisans), plumbers tearing up the sidewalk, pairs of American tourists with guidebooks and maps, children, artists from the Pensione Annalena, clerks, priests, housemaids with shopping baskets stopping to finger the furred rabbits hanging upside down outside the poultry shops, the sanitation brigade (a line of blue-uniformed men riding bicycles that propel wheeled platforms holding two or three garbage cans and a broom made of twigs), a pair of boys transporting a funeral wreath in the shape of a giant horseshoe, big tourist buses from abroad with guides talking into microphones, trucks full of wine flasks from the Chianti, trucks of crated lettuces, trucks of live chickens, trucks of olive oil, the mail truck, the telegraph boy on a bicycle, which he parks in the street, a tripe-vendor, with a glassed-in cart full of smoking-hot entrails, outsize Volkswagen station wagons marked 'U.S. Forces in Germany', a man on a motorcycle with an overstuffed armchair strapped to the front of it, an organ-grinder, horse-drawn fiacres from the Pitti Palace. It is as though the whole history of Western locomotion were being recapitulated on a single street; an aeroplane hums above; missing only is the Roman litter.

The Stones of Florence Mary McCarthy

Task 9

In her description of the Via Romana, which she uses as an example of a Florentine street, McCarthy employs a simple sentence structure. She uses adverbial elements in the first part of sentences, and she inverts the order of subject and verb, thus:

adverbial	**verb**	**subject**
Along the narrow sidewalk, single file,	*walks*	*a party* . . .

adverbial	**verb**	**subject**
Past them	*flows*	*a confused stream of* . . .

The rest of the second sentence above consists of a catalogue of traffic and people.

It is this varied and wonderful list that establishes and develops the sense of business in the street. McCarthy also uses the present participle throughout to emphasize the continuity of the activities she lists:

clinging to the buildings
wheeling in and out.

Go through the paragraph, and ring all the other examples of present participles used in this way.

In addition to using the present participle, McCarthy exploits the noun phrase in her catalogue:

a Rolls-Royce <u>with</u> a chauffeur and a Florence licence plate
American tourists <u>with</u> guidebooks
trucks full <u>of</u> wine flasks <u>from</u> the Chianti.

Underline the other examples of noun phrases in which prepositional post-modifiers are used.

McCarthy organizes the contents of her catalogue in this long sentence by alternating between vehicles and people. Add examples from the sentence to each of the blank spaces below.

vehicles   *grocery carts*

people   . . . .

vehicles   . . . .

people   . . . .

She concludes with a sentence which summarizes her theme:

It is as though the whole history of Western locomotion were being recapitulated on a single street . . .

Thus, the reader is reminded, at the end of a very long and densely-packed paragraph that the writer is not simply presenting a catalogue of things to be seen on a Florentine street; she is also taking the particular instance as an example of human diversity and historical development. The paragraph follows a pattern:

opening idea: the typical Florentine Street
development of idea: a description of people, traffic and activities
closing idea: the diversity represented in one Florentine street

Look back at your own description of a busy street. Did you make your viewpoint and theme clear to your reader? If not, could you rewrite the opening and closing sentences or add further sentences to make the theme clearer? Do you have to make other changes as a result of these amendments or additions?

3 Evoking an atmosphere

Task 1

Mary McCarthy's description of a Florentine street reveals the importance of theme in descriptive writing. Without a unifying idea, descriptive writing tends to be no more than that: a catalogue or a picture without a purpose.

Another feature of descriptive writing is viewpoint or attitude. The writer will tend to indicate what he or she thinks of the subject of the description. Indeed, the description may be presented in such a way as to illustrate the writer's reactions or feelings which may be related to a broader intention on the writer's part.

Good travel writing doesn't just describe; it also interprets. It will offer the reader insight into the writer's mind as well as an understanding of the places and people met during the writer's travels.

Imagine that you are travelling and that you have come to a town which is rather dilapidated. Cast your mind back to such a place within your own experience and make a mental journey through the town. Make notes of the things which you saw, trying to be as detailed as possible. Use all your senses: sight, hearing, smell and even taste and identify a feeling which the place evoked in you. Write down as many words as you can which are associated with this feeling.

Begin writing a description. Write as freely as you can, even in note form. Don't try to organize your thoughts — just let your thoughts wander on the main feeling that the place evoked.

Task 2

Now that you have a first draft, your task is to make it more effective. One way to add atmosphere and a sense of place is to use vocabulary which develops and reinforces feeling and mood. You can use nouns, adjectives, adverbs and phrases.

Go through your draft, and change existing vocabulary or add new items. Choose words which reinforce the mood or atmosphere you wish to create. To help do this, use a thesaurus.

Here is a reference for 'dilapidated' from *Roget's Thesaurus*. You will probably find some words here which would be useful in your description.

Check other words in the thesaurus for further useful vocabulary, e.g. 'moulder'.

---

dilapidated, the worse for wear, in ruins, in shreds; weather-beaten, decrepit, ruinous, ramshackle, tottery, tumbledown, on its last legs; slummy, condemned; worn, well-w., frayed, shabby, tatty, holey; seedy, down at heel 801 adj. *poor*; rusty, rotten, moss-grown, moth-eaten, worm-e., dog-eared 51 adj. *decomposed*.

    Vb. *deteriorate*, not improve, get no better; worsen, go from bad to worse; slip, slide, go downhill; not maintain 657 vb. *relapse*; fall off, slump, decline, wane, ebb, sink, fail 37 vb. *decrease*; retrograde 286 vb. *regress*; lapse 603 vb. *tergiversate*; degenerate, go to the bad, spoil oneself 934 vb. *be wicked*; collapse, break down, fall, totter 309 vb. *tumble*; wear out, age 131 vb. *grow old*; fade, wither, wilt, shrivel, perish, crumble, moulder, mildew, grow moss, grow weeds; bolt, run to seed; weather, rust, rot, decay 51 vb. *decompose*; spoil, stale, fust; putrefy, fester, suppurate, gangrene, sicken 651 vb. *be ill*; make things worse 832 vb. *aggravate*.

Task 3

Jonathan Raban in his solitary journey by boat down the Mississippi River, described in the book, *Old Glory*, came to a very down-at-heel town called Prairie Du Chien. *Text 4* is his description, with much of the descriptive language omitted.

Work with a partner and read the text.

Text 4

West Blackhawk Street was dominated by the . . . . hotel.

I couldn't make out what its name had been: eight wooden letters,

. . . . and . . . ., were still pinned at . . . .

angles to its facade. Once they'd been a . . . . sky-blue; now

only a few . . . . of paint adhere to the crevices in the grain.

They had the tantalising . . . . of an unfinished crossword

puzzle:

<u>O</u>   <u>T</u>   <u>C</u>   <u>W</u>

<u>O</u>   <u>HO</u>   <u>L</u>

I looked inside the window. The ceiling was . . . . in and

the timber reception desk was whitened with flakes of . . . .

plaster. An . . . . tubular chair stood in a

. . . . of carpet which had lost its pile. There were flowerpots

on the windowsill, but the plants inside them had . . . . long ago,

leaving . . . . bamboo stakes behind.

All down the street there was the same . . . . air of

. . . . In each . . . . store there

was a . . . . pile of cardboard boxes; . . . . mosquito

mesh . . . . out from door frames. Gokey's Meats and

Groceries was a . . . . ruin. . . . . metal plaques

bore advertising slogans at once chirpy and . . . . A Coca-Cola

logo from the 1940s had its message . . . . almost completely

away. Was it PAUSE. . . DRINK or PLEASE. . . DRINK? I couldn't tell.

HILLDALE MILK — DRINK THE UDDER KIND was clear; so was REACH

FOR SUNBEAM BREAD. Even the realtors' signs which hung outside these

places were beginning to . . . . and . . . .

Add words and phrases to the blank spaces. To help do this, refer
once again to a thesaurus. Here, by way of example, is one of the
references given in *Roget's Thesaurus* for 'derelict' meaning
'disused'.

---

674. Non-use − **N.** *non-use*, abeyance, suspension 677 n. *inaction*; non-availability 190 n. *absence*; stagnation 679 n. *inactivity*; forbearance, abstinence 620 n. *avoidance*; disuse 611 n. *desuetude*; waiver, surrender 621 n. *relinquishment*; uselessness, write-off 641 n. *inutility*; superannuation.

Adj. *unused*, out of order, unusable, unemployable 641 adj. *useless*; unutilized, unapplied, spare, extra; unspent, unconsumed 666 adj. *preserved*; unessayed, untried; in abeyance, suspended; unrequired 860 adj. *unwanted*; unemployed, idle 679 adj. *inactive*; briefless.

disused, derelict, discarded, cast-off, written off; laid up, out of commission, rusting; on the shelf, retired, super-annuated; obsolete, discredited 127 adj. *antiquated*.

Vb. *not in use*, hold in abeyance, have no use for; abstain, forbear 620 vb. *avoid*; dispense with, waive 621 vb. *relinquish*; overlook, disregard 458 vb. *neglect*; save, reserve, keep in hand 632 vb. *store*; decline 607 vb. *reject*.

disuse, leave off 611 vb. *disaccustom*; lay up, put in mothballs; lay aside; superannuate, pension off, put out to grass; discard, dump, ditch, scrap write off; jettison, throw overboard 300 vb. *eject*; slough, cast off 229 vb. *doff*; relinquish 779 vb *not retain*; suspend 752 vb. *abrogate*; discharge, lay off 300 vb. *dismiss*; drop, supersede, replace 150 vb. *substitute*.

Choose words from the list above and the lists given in Task 11 to
develop the sense of decay and lost prosperity which suffuses Rabin's
original description.

As you will have discovered, the effectiveness of Raban's description
derives not simply from his use of adjectives, although these are
important. He also uses nouns and verbs to add to the sense of
dereliction. And he makes an analogy between the partially
obliterated hotel sign and an incomplete crossword puzzle. This is
an arresting and apt analogy which adds to the sense of puzzlement
and disquiet which Raban felt at the time and which he is able to share
with his reader.

Return to your own descriptions and discuss any improvements you
could make in the light of your completion of Raban's description.

Task 4

Not all of the words which you used to complete the text in Task 12 will be correct or the most appropriate. However, the exercise will have made you think about what the best words might be. Now you can see what Raban actually wrote.

West Blackhawk Street was dominated by the dead hotel. I couldn't make out what its name had been: eight wooden letters, cracked and bleached, were still pinned at odd angles to its facade. Once they'd been a bright sky-blue; now only a few shreds of paint adhere to the crevices in the grain. They had the tantalising obscurity of an unfinished crossword puzzle:

$$\underline{O} \quad \underline{T} \quad \underline{C} \quad \underline{W}$$
$$\underline{O} \quad \underline{HO} \quad L$$

   I looked inside the window. The ceiling was falling in and the timber reception desk was whitened with flakes of rotten plaster. An abandoned tubular chair stood in a waste of carpet which had lost its pile. There were flowerpots on the windowsill, but the plants inside them had died long ago, leaving naked bamboo stakes behind.
   All down the street there was the same sad air of dereliction. In each vacated store there was a dusty pile of cardboard boxes; torn mosquito mesh peeled out from the door frames. Gokey's Meats and Groceries was a boarded ruin. Rusted metal plaques bore advertising slogans at once chirpy and wan. A Coca-Cola logo from the 1940s had its message eaten almost completely away. Was it PAUSE. . . DRINK or PLEASE. . . DRINK? I couldn't tell. HILLDALE MILK — DRINK THE UDDER KIND was clear; so was REACH FOR SUNBEAM BREAD. Even the realtors' signs which hung outside these places were beginning to rust and fade.

With a partner, discuss your own choices for the blanks in Task 3 compared with Raban's original language.

Write the vocabulary of dereliction that Raban uses around the central term, like this:

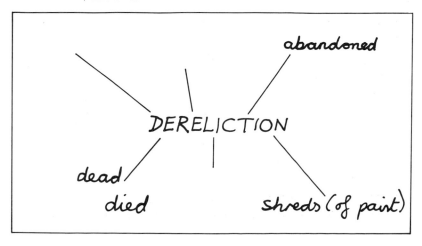

What you have is 'a field of meaning'. The use of related vocabulary reinforces the central idea or theme of the passage.

In Task 3, you read the description without these words. How does Raban's use of words from the same field of meaning develop and reinforce the theme of dereliction? Compare different choices at various places in the description to demonstrate the effect of using different words.

4   Making pictures in words

Task 1

In the last few tasks, you have concentrated on describing something sad and derelict. In the Raban passage, you saw how the theme of dereliction was developed through focusing on significant details, using a visual technique similar to that of the cinema in which a number of detailed shots are combined to produce a powerful image. Raban also uses a range of language items from the same area of meaning, thus reinforcing the atmosphere and his own reactions to it.

The same technique can be used, of course, to develop a theme of delight, pleasure, happiness and well-being, except that details and vocabulary will be different.

Choose a place which means a great deal to you in a positive sense. Identify a theme which this place can be used to illustrate or exemplify and quickly write down as many details as you can about the place. (Use the nutshelling procedure if you have difficulty in identifying a theme.)

Write a first draft describing the place and develop opening and closing statements to make the theme clear to the reader. Refine the expression by using a range of language related to your theme and viewpoint. Refer to a thesaurus for relevant vocabulary. Make lists of words in related fields, as you did in Section 2, and incorporate such words and phrases in your description. Reorganize your ideas and your text as new ideas or refinements suggest themselves.

Write a final draft, incorporating all the changes and improvements you have made. Omit the title.

Exchange texts with a partner. Suggest a suitable title for your partner's text. Discuss with your partner whether this title reflects the main idea which he or she is trying to communicate.

1 Introduction

In an earlier unit, 'Promoting an image,' you practised writing advertisements and you learnt about the importance of economy of expression since in advertisements the cost of advertising is generally related to the number of words in the text. Although all good writing tends to be economical, there is one type of writing in which economy is especially important — slogan writing for a competition.

Usually, in such competitions there is a stipulated length within which competitors are required to produce an effective statement linked to the product or service concerned. The constraints are similar to those within which advertising copywriters, journalists, and even poets must work.

Every word counts

2 Using words economically

Task 1

Individually, follow the instructions for the Olympus Portable Video System competition. Put all the 'entries' together. Read aloud and discuss each entry. Discuss which entries are best and why you think they are the best.

WIN AN **OLYMPUS** PORTABLE VIDEO SYSTEM

How to enter

Using your skill and judgement, examine the six special features of an Olympus Portable Video System listed below and place them in order of priority. For example, if you think that "the camera is easy to operate" is the most important consideration when buying a portable video system, then place E in box 1 on the Entry Form, and so on.

Then tell us, in an apt and original way, in not more than 10 extra words, why you would like to own an Olympus Portable Video System.

	OLYMPUS PORTABLE VIDEO SYSTEM FEATURES
A	The camera has a built-in microphone for live sound.
B	The system is light and portable.
C	The camera works in low light conditions.
D	The camera has a powerful zoom lens for close up or distant filming.
E	The camera is easy to operate.
F	The camera has automatic focusing.

ALPEN 'OLYMPUS' COMPETITION ENTRY FORM

Send your completed Entry Form to:
ALPEN 'OLYMPUS' COMPETITION,
P.O. Box 6, Kettering, Northants NN15 5JW,
to arrive by 30th June 1984.

	ENTRY
1	
2	
3	
4	
5	
6	

Name _____
(BLOCK LETTERS PLEASE)

Address _____

_____

_____

Age if under 18 ☐

Signed by Parent or Guardian _____

_____

I would like to own an Olympus Portable Video

System because _____

_____

_____ (Maximum 10 extra words)

Task 2

A good entry for this competition would probably highlight a feature or features of the product and present the information in a clever and memorable manner. How do these entries conform to these two criteria?

I would like to own an Olympus Portable Video System because . . .

it brings the past to the present.
it beats Dad's home movies.
it will go with me wherever I go.
it brings 'em back alive.
it captures living moments.
everyone can be her own film producer with Olympus.
it's a foolproof system for foolish filmers.
it's a sure-fire system for fumbling filmers.

Can you now improve on your own versions? What changes of ideas, vocabulary, sentence construction, etc. would you like to make to your own?

Check a thesaurus for vocabulary. For instance, if you took the contrasting ideas of 'success' and 'unskilful', as in the last examples above, you might find other words which would inspire new ideas. The following words are listed under 'proficient' (the next entry to 'unskilfulness'):

dab
virtuoso
master
crack shot

This might lead to a new completion such as:

it makes a virtuoso of even a novice.
with it a bad hand becomes a dab hand.

Task 3

In the Olympus competition, you had just ten words in which to make your winning point. In the next competition, you have just over twice as many words, but the topic is rather different. Read the 'How to Enter' instructions for the competition opposite.

Discuss with two other people what seem to be the best choices for the newlyweds. Make your own choice of item or items.

HOW TO ENTER

Claire and Paul are both in their 20s. Claire works in one of the big banks. Paul is a nurse. They have decided to settle out of London, and on the right you can see their brand-new living room. As with many young newlyweds, they could afford only the basics of furnishing and now the room looks sparse.

But you are going to change all that. From the selection of goodies shown on this page, we want you to spend up to £300 in the way that you think would best enhance their room as it stands. You may want to buy two or three big items, or go for lots of smaller ones. But remember, however many items you choose their total value must not exceed £300.

Then complete the coupon on page 21 and, in not more than 25 words, say which one item you think a newlywed pair could least do without, and why.

From the small pictures, marked A–K, and up to a value of £300, we want you to add to Claire and Paul's basic furniture above — which includes a TV, vase, books, tray, sofa and curtains.

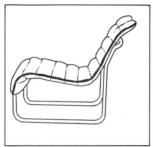

A £29, occasional chair, h:74cm, w:60cm, d:86cm

B £7.95, table lamp, h:30cm

C £11.95, light, h:27cm

D £29.95, storage unit, h:178cm, w:75cm; d:21cm

E £59, white/beech table, h:76cm, w:138cm, d:76cm

F £79, white desk, h:75cm, w:125cm, d:60cm

G £37.50, trolley, h:74cm, w:72cm, d:46cm

H £43.40, china, 4 settings of 9 pieces each

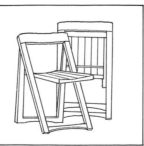

I £31.80, 4 folding chairs, h:79cm, w:45cm, d:55cm

J £13.95, stripy rug in blue/yellow/grey, 115cm×195cm

K £5.95, quartz clock

Task 4

Having made your choice, you need to consider what the basis of
your choice was. Was it convenience, comfort, luxury, common
sense, frivolity or something else?

Think of ideas associated with the basis of your choice and write
them down as they come to you. They may be associated with
activities, feelings or emotions.

Now consult a thesaurus for vocabulary connected to the associations
that you have listed. For instance, if you have listed 'convenience'
among your associations, you will find the following entry in *Roget's
Thesaurus*:

convenience
opportunity
euphoria
utility
expedience
leisure
facility.

Which of these terms will be most appropriate? Probably 'utility' will
be one of the terms to look up:

---

640. Utility — **N.** *utility*, use, usefulness; employability, serviceability, handiness 628 n. *instrumentality*; adaptability, applicability, suitability 642 n. *expedience* service, avail, help, stead 703 n. *aid*; value 644 n. *goodness*; virtue, capacity, potency 160 n. *power*; advantage, benefit; profitability, earning capacity 171 n. *productiveness*; profit 771 n. *gain*; convenience, benefit; utilization 673 n. *use*.

Adj. *useful*, of use, helpful of service 703 adj. *aiding*; sensible, practical, applied, functional; multipurpose, all-purpose; commodious, convenient 642 adj. *expedient*; handy, serviceable, fit for, good f., adaptable, applicable, usable, employable, good, valid; efficacious, effective 160 adj. *powerful*; pragmatic, utilitarian.

profitable, paying, remunerative 771 adj. *gainful*; prolific, fertile 164 adj. *productive*; beneficial, advantageous, to one's advantage, edifying, worth-while 615 adj. *good*; invaluable, priceless 644 adj. *valuable*.

Vb. *be useful*,—of use etc. adj.; avail, stead, stand one in good s.; come in handy, perform a function; serve, serve one's turn, suit one's purpose 642 vb. *be expedient*; help 703 vb. *aid*; do service, do yeoman s. 742 vb. *serve*; benefit 644 vb. *do good*; pay, make a profit.

In choosing vocabulary from such a list, you will need to keep in mind
two conflicting requirements — the need to be informal and the need
to keep within the stipulated number of words.
Some terms are more casual, e.g. *come in handy*, while others are
too formal, e.g. *expedient*. Your choice of vocabulary will have to be
made with care as, in general, slogans are informal in style.

Task 5

Use your notes and vocabulary lists to write the twenty-five word
text.

Task 6

With three or four fellow students, form a competition committee.
Discuss what you would expect to find in a winning entry and make a
list of the features you will look for.

Collect together a number of 'entries', making sure that none of the
entries belongs to members of the committee, and choose the
winner.

Collect together all the winners from each group. Read aloud each
winner, and from these select the winning entry.

Task 7

Discuss what it was that made the winning entry the best. Was it the
choice of item(s), the reasons given for choosing it or the use of
language? What was especially good or notable about the choice of
language?

3   Choosing vocabulary

Task 1

In the two competitions so far, there has been a word limit on the
entries. In the competition on page 82, there is no word limit, only
the instruction to 'write a short sentence'. This could be a trap for
the unwary. Although there is no word limit, it is easy to fall into the
trap of writing *too* much. Even here, brevity is important.

Study the details of the competition. Discuss with a partner the
clothes and the choice of clothes for each occasion specified. Discuss
the reasons you might have for liking next summer's fashions.

Task 2

Choose your own reason or reasons for liking the fashions. Follow a
similar procedure to the one suggested in Task 3. That is, think of
reasons, and then look up relevant terms in a thesaurus. For
instance, you might decide that *smart* is an appropriate term, but that
it is a little hackneyed for use in your sentence. Here is the entry for
smart in *Roget's Thesaurus*: (Two of the words — *pang* and *suffer* —
are not adjectives, so they can be rejected.)

smart
speedy
pang
intelligent
suffer
witty
fashionable

Which of these terms will be most appropriate? If you decide that
fashionable is the one to look up, you will find a range of adjectives,

Collect sizzling summer clothes for you and your man from the stores that sum up today's style

| FIRST PRIZE £2,000 |
| SECOND PRIZE £1,500 |
| THIRD PRIZE £1,000 |

PLUS seven lucky runners up win £500, all in vouchers valid right through the year to spend in any way you want at any Next store around the country.

Next's best news is that their fabulous fashion chain has moved into menswear. This means that their special blend of high fashion and affordable prices is now available to the man in your life. Around 90 Next men's shops are opening nationwide (Next have over 300 outlets altogether) with a summer collection that combines up-to-the-minute detailing with quality, finish and design.

The new season's summery look is packed with cool pastels, hot prints, smart suits and crisp navy and white combinations – all you both need to take you through the season to all sorts of places. Enter our competition and a Next summer wardrobe could be yours.

RULES OF ENTRY

Entrants must be 18 or over and may submit only one entry. Winners must be prepared to accept their prize in person or to nominate a representative on their behalf; be willing to have their names published and be interviewed if necessary. The decision of the judges, including the Editor, is final and no correspondence can be entered into. Employees of Next and the National Magazine Company Ltd and their relatives are not eligible to enter. The contest is open only to readers living in Great Britain and Northern Ireland and closes on 30 April 1985. Post this coupon now (or make a copy on a separate sheet if you do not want to cut your magazine) to GH Next Fashion Competition, PO Box 5, London SW16 5QH. Results will be published in a future edition of *Good Housekeeping* as soon as space permits, but this cannot be sooner than four months.

Fashion Editor/Angela Kennedy
Promotions Editor/Frances Barnes
Photographs/John Bishop
Make-up/Arianne
Hair/Stephen Carey at Michaeljohn

WHAT YOU HAVE TO DO

To win these sensational wardrobes, look at the collection of fabulous summer clothes in our photographs and imagine how they'd appeal to budget conscious young couples with plenty of interests and more fashion sense than cash. We would like you to team four different couples picking the clothes they would choose to go together on the events below. For instance, you might select couple A/1 to go to event (iii) and couple B/4 to go to event (i), and so on. Finally, write a short sentence saying what appeals most to you in Next's summer fashions.

	MAN	WOMAN
i) A river picnic party	☐	☐
ii) Open air summer concert with the boss	☐	☐
iii) A country cricket match and tea	☐	☐
iv) A day in town attending an antiques fair	☐	☐

NEXT'S SUMMER FASHIONS APPEAL TO ME BECAUSE

_____

_____

_____

_____

NAME   INITIALS MR/MRS/MISS
(Capital letters)

ADDRESS
(Capital letters)

_____

_____

      POSTCODE

POST COUPON TO NEXT COMPETITION, PO BOX 5, LONDON SW16 5QH.

A

B

C

D

1

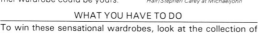

2

3

4

some of which will definitely not be appropriate, e.g. *foppish, high-stepping, swanky, dandified, braw*. But others may well be useful: *modish, stylish, well-dressed, well-groomed, tasteful, classy, up-to-the-minute, modern*.

Task 3

Decide on the theme which you wish to develop in your competition entry. You may find the events which are listed could provide a clue, e.g. the contrast between town and country, casual and formal. Select vocabulary appropriate to your theme and write a number of different entries in which you develop your main idea in a variety of ways, e.g. by contrast or comparison.

Finally, choose what you consider to be the best version. Hand it in anonymously to the teacher. Each entry will be read out and the class should choose the best one as the winner.

Task 4

Discuss what it was in the winning entry which made it the best and how other entries could have been improved.

Task 5

Now that you have completed several competitions, you can try to devise a competition of your own. Work with several others as a competition committee. Discuss the topics which you could set for a competition, remembering that the competition must include a written component. Prepare the information and instructions for the competition and discuss the criteria by which you will judge entries.

Exchange the completed information with another group. Complete the competition which you have been given and then return it to the competition setters. Discuss the entries you have received and choose a winner.

4 Mini-sagas

Task 1

In the previous exercises, you have written completions for competitions whose focus has been a commercial product. Not all competitions have such a commercial orientation, however. One competition with literary rather than commercial considerations was the 'Mini-saga Competition' organized by *The Sunday Telegraph*, a leading quality newspaper.

The aim of the competition was to write a story with a beginning, a middle and an end in exactly fifty words — no more and no less. An additional fifteen words were allowed for a title. There were nearly

50,000 entries, and below are the overall winner and the winning story in the under-eighteens category.

DIFFERENT VALUES, OR WHO GOT THE BEST OF THE BARGAIN?
by Reg Ferm
Harris boasts he gave an African a cheap watch for an uncut diamond. Sold it and gambled the proceeds for more. Abukali tells of the titik he swapped for a wife and two goats. Harris chases further millions. Abukali sleeps in the shade while his children tend his twenty goats.

WHAT THE SLEEPING BEAUTY WOULD HAVE GIVEN HER RIGHT ARM FOR
by Zoe Ellis
This princess was different. She was a brunette beauty with a genius of a brain. Refusing marriage, she inherited all by primogenesis. The country's economy prospered under her rule. When the handsome prince came by on his white charger, she bought it from him and started her own racehorse business.

Here is one written in class. It was not entered for the competition!

CARGO CULT
A booming noise descended and with it a boat from the skies landed in the lagoon. Later, strange pale creatures came ashore and, like gods, they scattered glittering cargo among us. Then they left us dreaming. Now we await their return. Alas, the sky is empty. Have the gods forgotten us?

Write a mini-saga of your own. You do not have to imitate any of the examples above. They are just examples to show you what is possible.

Use your imagination. You don't have to write about anything within your own experience. In fact, the less your saga is based on your own experience, the better, because writing the saga should involve imagination. Also, remember — economy of language is essential because you have only fifty words (plus up to fifteen for a title). You also have a time deadline: 15 minutes.

When you have finished, read your saga to members of your group and discuss each other's sagas. Improve your saga or rewrite it.

For further practice, work together with a partner on a different saga. Does the saga written by two people differ from the saga written by one person alone?

If you wish, you could make writing a mini-saga a regular competition either within your class or between classes. It is a very effective way of focusing your writing and developing discipline in all aspects of writing from generating ideas to expressing yourself with economy and effectiveness.

1 Introduction

In this unit, you will follow a slightly different sequence of activities than in other units. Even so, discussion with other students will be important. Of equal importance will be the use of all your senses to recall experiences and sensations so as to provide the details which are crucial in conveying a sense of actuality to your reader.

In addition to 'brainstorming', you will do the activity called 'nutshelling' which was introduced in Unit 7. In nutshelling you progressively summarize ideas so as to identify the main theme of the essay which you will write.

2 Producing and organizing ideas

Step 1

Read Text 1 which is an extract from *The Sunday Times* of 20 January 1985.

Do you have any memories associated with food and drink? Write down as many memories and associations as you can. Don't worry about logic or correctness. These notes are for your eyes only!

Step 2

Stuck? Close your eyes and think of memories to do with the sight, the smell, the feel, the taste of food or drink. Write down all the ideas that come to you.

Text 2 (which continues on page 85) is an example of some random ideas which were jotted down one hot morning in Indonesia when doing this activity. The ideas are random, though they do reflect the fact that the writer was in a foreign place. Also, they only really mean something to the person who wrote them. As ideas for an essay to be read by someone else, they are as yet in a primitive state and will need a lot of reworking.

Text 2

> hot and spicy curry
> curry glowing down my throat and into my stomach!
> coconut cream in curry
> 'taro' — smoky flavour from the 'lovo'
> cassis sorbet
> sunny hot vine-shaded meal
> river outside
> languorous days in the sun — food and sleep
> ratatouille — the mixtures of vegetables, garlic,
>   oil and herbs

10
Memories

Text 1

Taste of nostalgia

WE ASKED readers to tell us the memories that food conjured up. Here is a short selection from the letters that poured in:

Jessica Boote, Tankerton, Kent. . . . Oysters and champagne remind me of the time my mother was ill and my worried father wanted her to eat *anything*. She couldn't manage much and we finished it off, making me an expensive girlfriend through the years.

Francis Jarvis, London Road, Leicester. . . . A sniff of methylated spirits reminds me of crab sandwiches in a beach hut.

W. K. Doughty, Beverley, East Yorkshire. . . . Fat bacon brings memories of a small south Lincolnshire farm where pigs wandered at will.

T. Williamson, Haltwhistle, Northumberland. . . . Today's roasting chicken, with its slightly fishy smell, reminds me, unluckily, of the delectable chicken my mother used to roast in her wood-fired oven. There should be a society for the preservation of epicurean delights.

> fish - on the fire - peel off the skin - moist juicy flesh -
> coral sand
> cheese - the salty muttony flavour of roquefort
> saté - hot & sizzling and peanut sauce
> the strange and suspicious texture of vegetarian 'meat'
> Japanese food - visual arrangement - nothing is
> what it seems
> raw fish - Japanese
> Pacific islands
> sushi - rice and bits of fish & raw ginger

Step 3

Discuss your memories with a partner. You don't have to show your partner your notes. Simply talk about the ideas in your notes. Compare your memories and associations and note down any other memories or associations or ideas that come to you as you compare experiences.

Step 4

What were the circumstances associated with your memories of food or drink? Take one or two of the items you have listed and make a further list of the circumstances associated with the food. Think of the time, the place, the people and the occasion. Write down any ideas that come to you.

Step 5

Are you stuck? Think of one of the circumstances and list all of the associations that have to do with sounds, sights, smells and feelings or emotions. Now talk about these ideas with a partner and note down any new ideas that come to mind as you and your partner discuss experiences.

Step 6

Take one of your experiences and all the notes that you have made. Begin writing about it. Write quickly. Don't worry about correct grammar or sentences. Don't make any corrections as you write. If you get stuck, look at the notes that you have made. When you have written 5 or more lines, read over what you have written. What is the main idea in what you have written? Summarize that idea in a statement that contains the main point or essence of what you have written.

Step 7

Begin writing again. This time, begin with the statement you wrote at the end of the previous step. Do this procedure twice more.

Text 3 is an example of what was done with the notes and ideas on food from Step 2, following this procedure.

Text 3

For me food is associated with exotic places. My main memories of food are associated with places like France, Italy, Turkey and Asia and the Pacific. In particular, it is the flavour of food which is evocative, together with the smell.

The flavour and smell of food is linked with foreign places. When I smell a particular combination of tomatoes and garlic, I think of Italy. When I smell coconut, I think of Fiji and the tropics. And when I smell vanilla, I think of the patisseries in France.

The smell of food is the most evocative sensation associated with food. It always acts as a powerful stimulus to memory — to occasion, circumstance, feeling. When I smell coconut, I always think of back to arriving in Suva, Fiji, when the aroma of coconut used to hang over one part of the town by the docks.

While the smell of food evokes memories, taste is also important. Figs on a hillside in Tuscany. The paper thin smoothness of prosciutto matched with the sandy texture of ripe figs. The melting smoothness of canelloni with a creamy sauce — food that seemed to melt into one's mouth with an almost sublime combination of taste and texture. The unexpected pungent contrast of roast pork and fennel. The combination of garlic and olive oil and spaghetti — simplicity with superb 'I can't eat enough of it' flavour.

The taste, texture and aroma of food form powerful stimuli to memory. And then there are the circumstances. Eating spaghetti and drinking wine in a vast kitchen in a stone-built house overlooking vineyards. Eating beneath the vines by the side of the Rhone — the light filtered through the leaves, as if living in an impressionist painting. And the river glinting and slipping past.

Many of my associations with food are linked to foreign places.

Step 8

Are you stuck? Continue writing, but write as if you were talking aloud to yourself. When you get stuck or reach a dead end, use your 'second voice' to get the conversation moving.

Step 9

Now you should have a lot of notes and some partly written paragraphs. Take the main ideas from your notes so far and rephrase them into a statement which can form the main idea for your essay. Write this statement down. Here is the main idea which was derived from the notes in Step 2: *Food means foreign places*

Now decide who you are going to write the essay for. Next, start a new draft of your essay, using the main idea as the linking theme. Refer to your notes and ideas to continue the essay.

Starting an essay can be very difficult, so here are five ways in which you could begin.

Method	*Example*
Factual statement	The average human being needs 2,500 calories a day to maintain energy and body weight.
Action	The waiter placed the dish in front of us with a flourish.
Dialogue	'I'm afraid that the asparagus is not on the menu this evening, but I can recommend the courgette flowers stuffed with salmon mousse.'
Anecdote	One evening in Argentina, as we were travelling from O'Brien to Buenos Aires, we stopped at this little roadside restaurant and . . .
Proverb or quotation	'Tell me what you eat, and I will tell you what you are.' Brillat-Savarin
	'What is food to one man is bitter poison to others.' Lucretius

If you get stuck once you have begun writing, either use some of the idea-generating procedures you used in earlier steps or refer to Texts 4 and 5 to see how other people have written about memories of food and drink.

Step 10

Exchange drafts with a partner. Read each other's drafts and discuss what you have written and why you wrote it. Ask each other questions and ask for clarification, expansion, explanation. Use the comments to improve what you have written, and then write a final draft.

Step 11

If you haven't referred to Texts 4 and 5, read them now.

How did the writer of each text handle the theme of food and drink and memories and associations?

Step 12

Read Text 4 and discuss these questions with a partner.
- How does the writer of the coffee text use details of description and narrative to create a vivid impression? Make a list of the details of setting, utensils, food and events.
- What link does the writer make between coffee and ritual?
- How can you identify the sex of the writer? What particular detail enables you to say whether the writer is a man or a woman?
- What kind of publication do you think that the text is taken from?
- Who would the readers of such a text probably be?

Text 4

I have loved coffee ever since, as young children in Cairo, we waited outside my parents' bedroom door for signs of their awakening. When the shadows on the frosted glass began to move, a signal and an invitation to come in, we pounced and raced for the coveted places in the large double bed where we waited for the coffee ritual to start.

Maria, our Yugoslav nanny and housekeeper, brought in a large brass tray ornately engraved in praise of Allah, on which were placed five small cups in delicate bone china with gold arabesques near the rim. A glass of water held a piece of ice chipped from the block in the ice box, and was scented with a drop of orange flower water. A small plate carried a pile of oriental petits fours filled with dates, pistachios or ground almonds. My father poured out the coffee from two small copper *kanaks* (or *ibriks* as they are called in Turkish) with much ceremony, carefully shaking his hand so as to drop a little of the much prized froth in each cup. We passed the water round, then drank the syrupy black brew in little sips and with much reverence.

In Egypt, no one thought children should not drink coffee. It was usually assumed that we would like it sweet, and it was made accordingly and served with home-made preserves and jams. When we had finished, we turned over the tiny cups, for at least one member of the company was reputed to be good at fortune telling. Everything could be read in the grounds: travels, unexpected bequests, weddings. Sometimes the image of a bride-groom-to-be would be seen faintly in the gentle trickle of muddy powder.

My first and favourite coffee was Turkish coffee. Later, travels through Europe and schooldays in France introduced me to *café espresso* and *café filtre*.

Coffee C. Roden

Step 13

In Steps 2 and 7, you were given some first notes from a brainstorming session and some 'nutshelled' paragraphs. Now you can read the final version of the essay based on the earlier notes and paragraphs. Compare the notes with the final version.

- How were ideas in the notes and nutshelled paragraphs incorporated in the final version?
- Were all the ideas used? Or were many rejected?
- What was the main theme of the essay?
- How was the theme developed in the essay?
- How were the beginning and end of the essay linked together?

Text 5

'Carne ou ave?' I looked up. This was an offer I had never received before. She stood there in her plaid skirt, her white blouse with a bow at her neck. Beside her stood a trolley and in it were stacked regimented containers of food — beef or chicken.

I can't remember the choice I made, because, as with most airline meals, it was hardly memorable. Nor do I remember the exact location — probably somewhere between Rio and Buenos Aires. But, like many meals in the air, it was the prelude to another succession of exotic gastronomic experiences on the ground, because, for me, food means foreign places.

A whiff of tomato and garlic and I am in Italy, a country where the simplicity of the food is matched by the dignity and sense of occasion with which it is served, even in the humblest circumstances. For Italy is a land in which *carne* or even *ave* used to be scarce, while oil and flour and tomatoes were comparatively plentiful. Result: pasta and a range of dishes exploiting the resources of noodles, oil and tomato sauce — simple ingredients from which memorable meals could be made.

'Buon appetito!' We begin to eat. Malolo has prepared *spaghetti alla putanesca*. The kitchen is still redolent of the olive oil and garlic which form the sauce. Around me are my friends — a temporary family in a foreign place. Most of them, too, are exiles, but happily so in this contented corner of Northern Italy.

Outside the Tuscan sun vibrates over a landscape devoted entirely to vines. The grapes swell and ripen. Meanwhile, inside, we raise our glasses of local wine to the cook. Or strictly, tumblers, since we are dining with that mixture of simplicity and opulence that characterizes Italy. The simplicity of garlic and oil and spaghetti, the opulence of taste and texture. After all, when one has oil and garlic, wine and spaghetti, sunshine and fellowship, who needs *carne ou ave?*

Step 14

Review your own notes and essay and incorporate any improvements suggested by your study of Texts 4 and 5.

Writing reports

1 Introduction

For many people, writing reports is an important and regular part of their work. Although reports tend to be conventional in organization and style, the processes which go into writing a report are similar to those used in any type of writing. These processes include:

generating ideas
identifying a purpose
obtaining a clear idea of your audience
organizing ideas clearly and logically
discussing findings and conclusions
planning, drafting and rewriting
writing a final draft for the reader.

There are three main types of report.

Eye witness reports
These give an account of what was actually seen or experienced (e.g. a report of an accident or near accident).

Work reports
These are of three kinds:
a Progress reports on work as it goes on
b Completion reports on final progress
c Single work reports on work of limited scope or duration.

Investigation reports
These are of two kinds:
a Information reports, detailing and analysing findings and showing their significance
b Recommendation reports, advising on action to be taken as well as giving information.

In this unit, we shall be concerned with the two types of investigation reports.

2 From brief to draft

Task 1

A report conventionally contains the following parts:

a Title
b Terms of reference
c Proceedings
d Findings
e Conclusions
f Recommendations

Match the parts of a report with the descriptions below.

☐ 1 What you think about the information
☐ 2 What you were asked to investigate, who instructed you and when the report is required
☐ 3 What you think should be done
☐ 4 The information or facts
☐ 5 What you did to obtain information and facts
☐ 6 What the report is about

Some reports may contain other parts:

Table of contents (for long reports only)
Summary (the key points and main aim of the report)
List of symbols, abbreviations and definitions
Discussion, analysis and argument, leading to conclusions
Acknowledgements (people who helped)
References (documents and published material which you consulted)
Appendices (for tables, figures, graphs, questionnaires).

In Unit 3, 'Reporting speech,' you dealt with anecdotes and stories whose purpose is to entertain. In such stories, the point is usually delayed until the end so as to maintain the reader's interest. By contrast, a report is usually written to inform and advise the reader. So, it is usually organized according to a 'pyramid of information', in which the point and purpose of the report are given at the beginning.

Title & summary   Most readers

Focus & orientation

Body of report

Most detailed   Few readers
information

The idea of such an arrangement is that it makes information required by the majority of readers most readily accessible — readers can stop reading when they have obtained as much detail as they need.

Task 2

In small groups, discuss the following questions:

• Which of the three kinds of reports listed in the introduction have you written in your job?
• Which kinds of reports might you be asked to write?
• Who would ask you?
• Why would they want a report?
• Who would read the report?

Summarize your discussion, and then compare notes with other groups. Write a summary of the main points in note form.

Task 3

One of the most important steps in writing a report is the briefing which the writer is given. The briefing gives the terms of reference for the report; in other words, the writer is told by whom the report is commissioned, for whom it is being prepared, why it is being written and when it is to be finished.

Here is an example of a report brief, presented in the form of a memorandum:

```
From:    Director
To:      Director of Studies

Please prepare a report on the recruitment of students during the period
1st July to 30th September this year and last year.  Would you pay special
attention to the relationship between student nationalitites and promotion
of courses in the countries from which the students have been recruited?
And could you note any changes from last year to this year?  No recommendations
are required.  The report is to be presented to the next Management Committee
meeting.
```

In a small group, write a brief for another group. The report is to be about report writing in your class and it is to be for your teacher. No recommendations are required.

Exchange the briefs and discuss the brief you have been given. Is it clear? Does it give you an objective? If the brief is not clear, ask the group who wrote it to give you more information and then finalize the brief.

Task 4

Now you have a brief for a report. The next step is to obtain some information. There are at least three ways in which you can find information:

- by referring to written material (e.g. previous reports, magazine and journal articles, books)
- by asking people for information (questionnaires, surveys, conversations and discussions)
- by looking and asking for yourself (investigation and field work).

In a small group, discuss what information you will need and where or to whom you will go for the information. (Note: You already have some information in note form as a result of the discussion in Task 2.) Compare your ideas with those of other groups.

Task 5

Using some of the information-gathering ideas you developed in Task 4, find out about report writing in your class. Keep notes of your findings.

Task 6

Now that you have obtained some data (or information), you can organize it. To do so, use these questions:

- Which are the important or significant facts?
- Which facts are interconnected?
- Do any of the facts contradict each other?
- Are there any trends in the information (e.g. that few people have to write recommendation reports)?
- What conclusions are you being lead to?

You may discover that you have to find out some more information in a particular area.

Next, you should group your information into sections according to the list given in the Introduction.

Task 7

The next step is to draft the report.

The Introduction (or terms of reference) will state what the report is about, who asked for it to be written, who the report is to be given to and when it is to be ready.

The main body can be organized according to:

chronological order (like a narrative of events)
spatial order (as in a description of a place)
descending order of importance (probably the most useful)
ascending order of complexity (from known to unknown)
or a combination of all of these.

Finally, the identity of the reader(s) should be kept in mind. You should ask yourself these questions about your readers while you plan and write your report.

- Are they alike or are they a mixed group?
- What do they already know about the subject?
- What do they need to know?
- How do they feel about the subject?
- What will they do with the information in the report?

If you are writing for a reader who already knows a lot about the subject, you will need to include very little background information in your report. If, however, you are writing for a very wide audience, whose background knowledge cannot be taken for granted, you will have to include more such information in your report.

It is also very important to realize that different readers will have different interests. So, different readers may require different reports, even when the same general area is being dealt with.

Match the readers in the first column to the information in the second column. (Some information will be of interest to more than one reader.)

Readers	*Information*
1 teachers	a difficulties in writing reports
2 students	b length and lay-out
3 typists	c the cost of writing a report
4 businesspeople	d students' views on report writing
	e methods of teaching report writing
	f textbooks for teaching report writing
	g the use of word processors for report writing

Next, in your small group, draft the report, keeping all of the above points in mind.

Task 8

Exchange drafts with another group. Discuss each other's drafts with these questions in mind:
- Is the information clearly organized?
- Does it make sense to the potential reader?
  (Although the reader is your teacher, he or she will probably not actually know very much about the report writing experience of your class, which is the subject of your report.)
- Do you distinguish clearly between fact (as given in the proceedings and findings sections) and opinion (in the conclusions section)?

Task 9

Now it is time to write a final draft. This draft should benefit from the discussion in Task 8. In addition, you should now give some consideration to expression.

Avoid a conversational or journalistic style, e.g.

You may ask, 'When do students write reports?' Our reply is, 'Very rarely.'

Do not be too formal, e.g.

An investigation into the report writing habits of students was commissioned.

Avoid using a lot of passive voice constructions, e.g.

A survey was carried out.

Use active constructions and simple vocabulary if possible, e.g.

We did a survey among students.

When you have finished the final draft, read it carefully, and make any necessary corrections before giving it to your teacher.

3   Making recommendations

Task 1

As a class, discuss the reports which you have written on report writing. Suggest what recommendations could be made, based on the conclusions of your reports. Write these recommendations in the following form:

```
RECOMMENDATIONS

We recommend that

a) _____ should be _____

b) _____ should be _____
```

It is often best to give recommendations in a list, each item being separately numbered.

Task 2

On pages 98 and 99 is a report dealing with ways of using an empty room in a school. It is a *recommendation* report, based on a survey of suggestions made by staff and students.

Read the report and list any missing information, keeping in mind the purpose and audience of the report. Finish the incomplete Recommendations section. To do this, you will need to discuss the earlier sections of the report, especially the Conclusions.

I. TERMS OF REFERENCE

To recommend ways of using of Room 1.1.

A sub-committee, consisting of the Director of Studies and the Administrative Assistant, was requested to undertake a survey at the staff meeting of 2nd July and was asked to report back to the staff meeting of 3rd September.

II. PROCEEDINGS

We circulated a questionnaire to all teaching staff and to a representative of the students. In addition, we visited two language schools Eurilex and Vitalang to find out about their resource and recreation facilities. Twenty-three out of thirty-two teaching staff returned completed questionnaires, while the students representative returned a report based on an informal survey of students' views.

III. FINDINGS

1. Questionnaire: Staff

The results of the teacher questionnaire are as follows:

Suggested use	Number
Staff resource centre (no 1 student access)	11
Staff & student resource centre	5
Listening library (audio & video for student use)	3
Student library	2
Overflow classroom	1
'Don't know'	1
	23

2. Survey: Students

The student representative reported the following suggestions which were equally popular among the students:

a) 'Quiet' room for students to read magazines, books.
b) Self-study centre for students
c) Project room, with magazines, books, tapes, and other resources for student use

A minority view was that the room could be used 'for staff purposes', which included a store room for materials and books.

3. Other Schools

Our visits to two other language schools showed that

a)   where adequate storage and management facilities exist, there is little value in having an additional resource centre for staff use only
b)   Self-access centres are underused by students
c)   A work space for students use is highly valued and much used, especially when project work is part of their course
d)   Permanently converting a room to a restricted use is not advisable

IV. CONCLUSIONS

1. Staff Views

There is no clear-cut majority in favour of staff-only use of the room. Although nearly half of the staff were in favour of the room being used for a staff-only resource centre, an equal number opted for using the room for a purpose which would involve student access.

2. Student Views

The students on the whole preferred a use for the room which would involve them and which would not restrict the room to staff-only use.

3. Other Schools

The experience of other schools shows that flexibility of use is important and that it is crucial to provide facilities which jointly benefit both staff and students.

The overall implications of the survey are that

a)   restricted use of such a room would not be popular

b)   student priorities are important when allocating such free space.

V. RECOMMENDATIONS

We recommend that

a) _____

_____

b) _____

_____

c) _____

_____

Signed: J R Heatherington
Director of Studies

A B Moire
Administrative Assistant

Task 3

The report you have just studied is not a very large one. When a report is longer than the example given here, it is advisable to write a summary. The summary is usually based on the conclusions and recommendations. In general, it is best to write an *informative* summary because it gives the reader a quick overview of the report, it focuses attention on the main aim of the report and it reinforces the main ideas. By contrast, a descriptive summary simply tells the reader about the report — it doesn't tell the reader what the report actually contains.

Here are examples of summaries of a report. Which one is more informative and helpful?

Summary A

This report describes a survey of report writing among students. The views and experience of students were obtained by questionnaire and interviews. General trends were shown and these are summarized. A number of recommendations are made with a view to improving the teaching of report writing.

Summary B

A survey of report writing among students showed that a majority had difficulty with organizing ideas, drawing conclusions and expressing themselves appropriately. Many students stated that their lack of familiarity with report writing conventions was a further problem. It is recommended that a new course should be prepared to deal with these problems.

Write an informative summary for the report on using Room 1.1.

4   Writing a report

Task 1

Work together with a partner or in a small group. Choose one of the report topics given below and write a brief for the topic you have chosen. (Refer to Task 3)

Find or produce information. This could involve asking other students for their views, or else imagining appropriate information.

Organize your information. (See Task 6)
Draft the report. (See Tasks 7 and 8)
Write a final draft. (See Task 9)

When you have written your final draft, exchange reports with other groups and evaluate each other's reports. Use these questions as a basis:

- Is the report clearly organized?
- Is the aim of the report clearly stated?
- Are the knowledge and requirements of the readers taken into account?
- Is the information presented in a relevant and easily understood way?
- Are all the relevant facts covered?
- Do the conclusions logically follow from the facts?
- Are the recommendations feasible and sensible?
- Is the expression clear and appropriate?

Report topics
1   A benefactor has given a sum of money to your school/college. It is equivalent to the cost of a new small car, such as a Fiat Uno or a Renault 5. One condition of the gift is that both students and staff must be involved in deciding how the money is to be used. A further condition is that the money must be spent on permanent and tangible things.

   You have been asked by the principal of the school to survey the views of staff and students and to present him with an information report.

2   You are secretary of a club. The club needs to extend its premises. The local authority has just made an offer of a building at a nominal rental. However, because of redevelopment plans, the building is likely to be available for only two or at most three years. Write a report to the club committee on the offer. Recommend action.

3   You are a member of an organization — it could be a school, a club or a company — which requires some new equipment. You have been asked to survey the available equipment and to recommend the best purchase. Your report is to go to the committee or the person who deals with purchasing.

4   Your organization has been asked to amalgamate with a rival
    organization. The proposed amalgamation is controversial. As
    secretary of your organization, you have been asked to present
    the management committee with a report recommending the
    most appropriate response to the approach from the rival
    organization.

5   You are secretary of an organization which holds an annual
    international conference. You have been asked to prepare a
    report recommending a venue for the conference which is to
    be held in two years' time.

1 Introduction

Short story writers have a formidable task: within a limited number of words, they have to create characters, present a narrative and develop a theme. Unlike novelists, short story writers have to achieve all of these things in a brief compass and in such a way that the reader's interest will be engaged right from the start. Furthermore, in one form of the short story — such as the one discussed here — there will be an unexpected twist so that there will be a 'sting in the tail'. Given these constraints, it is scarcely any wonder that really good short story writers are rare.

One such writer was Somerset Maugham. How did he construct a short story? How did he sustain the reader's interest? How did he employ the resources of the language? These are questions which this unit will attempt to answer. And in answering them, it may help you to develop some short story writing skills of your own.

12

Writing short stories

2 Developing a storyline

Task 1

Text 1
It is always easier to eat things if you know what they are called, or better, if you know what they are made of. There was no cosmological structure in Mahalingham's meal, at least none that could make sense to a Western mind. To begin with what looked like beef rissoles in black sauce and find them to be piercingly sweet cakes in honey was disconcerting. I mean, a Western banquet recapitulates the history of the earth from primal broth through sea beasts to land predators and flying creatures and ends with evidence of human culture in cheese and artful puddings. Mahalingham's meal was all brutal surprises.

Earthly Powers Anthony Burgess

Have you ever eaten a meal which was 'all brutal surprises'? With three other people, talk about meals you have eaten — particularly meals which contained unexpected dishes or food which you could eat only with difficulty.

Did the unexpected or difficult food cause you any embarrassment? If so, how did you manage the situation? Or didn't you?

Task 2

Anthony Burgess characterizes the Western banquet as recapitulating the history of the earth. In other words, a typical western meal has a structure and sequence.

Set out below is the menu of a meal served by a European airline. The sequence of courses is muddled. With a partner, put the courses into the conventional order.

Text 2

DINNER

Morello Cherry Pie

French Beans and Carrots

Cheese and Biscuits

Coffee

Smoked Trout with Tarragon Dressing

Tournedos Rossini

Chocolate Mints

Parisienne Potatoes

Usually, when we eat in a restaurant, we work through the sequence of courses, beginning with soup or fish, and ending with cheese and 'artful puddings.' Courses can be omitted for reasons of appetite or economy.

If you were dining out, which of the courses in Text 2 could you omit without appearing to be odd or rude?

Task 3

Meals are usually social occasions. Often a meal is the occasion for a reunion at which old friends meet again and recall old times. Sometimes a meal may be an occasion for discussing business or making acquaintances.

With three other people, discuss occasions when you have taken part in a meal which was also a social occasion. How did you enjoy the meal? What did people talk about? What do you remember most about the occasion: the food, the other people, the setting, the conversation?

Write down any ideas or words that come to mind when you recall the occasion concerned.

Describe the food but avoid using adjectives like *delicious*. Compare the food to other things for colour, taste and smell, for example:

The salad had the crisp greenness of a spring landscape.
The fruit terrine was arranged with the geometrical elegance of a stained glass window.

3   Creating a structure

Task 1

When eating out in a restaurant, there are conventions about ordering and paying for the meal. Customs differ from country to country. Discuss these questions with three other people.

- What is the normal situation in your own country when dining out?
- Who pays for the meal?
- Is it common for a woman to entertain a guest (either man or woman) to a meal?
- What happens if a woman does entertain someone to a meal in a restaurant?
- Who orders the food and the wine?
- How is the meal presented to the diners?
- Is there any advice you would give to a foreigner dining out in your country?
- Have you ever been embarassed when dining out in a restaurant? For instance, have you ever found that you couldn't pay the bill? Did you find that you or a guest didn't like the food or the wine? What did you do?

Task 2

Work with a partner. One of you is A, the other is B. Read your own role card and act out the role play with your partner.

Person A	Person B
A person you have never met comes to your town. He or she is a friend of a friend. The visitor phones and suggests that you meet for lunch. You feel under an obligation to entertain the visitor to a meal, but you don't have much money. Your visitor suggests going to a rather expensive restaurant and proceeds to order the most expensive dishes on the menu. • Do you show your discomfort? • How do you avoid spending more money than you have? • How does the meal end?	You are visiting a town where you have an introduction to the friend of a friend. You phone this person, and suggest that you meet for lunch at a restaurant you have heard of. It serves specialities of the region. You arrange to meet, and at the restaurant, you order a very good meal, but you notice that your acquaintance seems rather ill at ease. You are not sure why. • What do you do? • How do you try to put your host/hostess at ease? • How does the meal end?

Find another partner, and tell each other about the lunch you have just had. Tell your new partner about what you and your friend ate. Describe the food. Discuss the financial and social difficulties of the situation.

Task 3

A meal as a social occasion can be used as the basis for a short story. A short story will usually have:

a setting, e.g. a restaurant or a house
characters, e.g. a host or hostess and a guest or guests
dialogue, both direct and reported
a story, i.e. the events that happened
a theme or main idea, e.g. reunions, being embarrassed, keeping up appearances
an unexpected ending
form, i.e. organization or shape to the story.

The story will usually be told from one viewpoint, and it may be in the first or third person. The extract from *Earthly Powers* was told in the first person.

With a partner, discuss how you could turn your role play into a short story.

- Would you tell it in the first or third person?
- What things can you do with first person narrative which you cannot do with third person, and vice versa?
- How would you begin your story?
- How could you use the organization of the meal to give form to the story?
- How would you end the story?
- How would you build up the characters?
- How would you maintain your reader's interest in the story right to the end?

Task 4

Using the ideas you discussed in Task 3, write a short story of about one thousand words. The short story is to be centred round a meal, and you can use the role play you did in Task 2 as a basis, together with the other ideas you developed in earlier exercises. Give your short story a title of no more than five words. Circulate stories among your group and compare and discuss them.

4   Arousing interest and anticipation

In this section, it is suggested that you work together with a partner and that you discuss the points that are dealt with in each task.

Task 1

As you may have discovered, writing a good short story is quite difficult, even when you have already thought out a story, characters and structure. The first problem is how to capture the interest of the reader.

Text 3, Part 1 is the opening paragraph of a short story by
W. Somerset Maugham. It is entitled *The Luncheon.*

Text 3
Part 1
I caught sight of her at the play and in answer to her beckoning I went
over during the interval and sat down beside her. It was long since I had
last seen her and if someone had not mentioned her name I hardly think I
would have recognized her. She addressed me brightly.

'Well, it's many years since we first met. How time does fly! We're none
of us getting any younger. Do you remember the first time I saw you? You
asked me to luncheon.'

Did I remember?

Which pronouns does Maugham use? Why does he use 'she' and 'her'
instead of naming the women? Normally, pronouns refer back to
someone or something either mentioned previously or known to both
speaker/writer and listener/reader. When a writer begins a story
with a pronoun, the reader does not share the reference with the
writer. The only way to find out who the referent might be is to read
on. Thus, the reader's interest is aroused.

Another technique is to manipulate time. Maugham begins his story
in the recent past:

I caught sight of her . . .

He then shifts to an earlier past:

It was a long time since I had last seen her . . .

And then he indicates a flashback with the question:

Did I remember?

The answer to the question is in Part 2.

Part 2
It was twenty years ago and I was living in Paris. I had a tiny apartment in
the Latin Quarter overlooking a cemetery and I was earning barely
enough money to keep body and soul together.

The reader then learns that the woman was passing through Paris
and wished to meet him, as she had just read a book of his. She
suggested that they have lunch at a very superior restaurant which
'was so far beyond my means that I had never even thought of going
there.' However, he agrees, and decides that if he economizes, he
should be able to pay for the luncheon and to cover his living
expenses for the next month.

They meet. In Part 3 he describes the woman, about whom the
reader will now feel some curiosity.

Part 3
She was not so young as I expected and in appearance imposing rather
than attractive. She was in fact a woman of forty (a charming age, but not

one that excites a sudden and devastating passion at first sight), and she gave me the impression of having more teeth, white and large and even, than were necessary for any practical purpose. She was talkative, but since she seemed inclined to talk about me I was prepared to be an attentive listener.

Underline all the adjectives Maugham uses in describing the woman. List her physical features.
- What impression does the description convey?
- Why does he particularly refer to her teeth?

Task 2

Maugham has now introduced:

the characters: himself and an unnamed woman
the setting: an expensive restaurant in Paris some time ago
the purpose of the meeting: to have a sociable lunch.

He has also established the fact that he was not very well off. How does the story continue? Read on.

Part 4
I was startled when the bill of fare was brought, for the prices were a great deal higher than I had anticipated. But she reassured me.
   'I never eat anything for luncheon,' she said.
   'Oh, don't say that!' I answered generously.
   'I never eat more than one thing. I think people eat far too much nowadays. A little fish, perhaps. I wonder if they have any salmon.'
   Well, it was early in the year for salmon and it was not on the bill of fare, but I asked the waiter if there were any. Yes, a beautiful salmon had just come in, it was the first they had had. I ordered it for my guest. The waiter asked her if she would have something while it was being cooked.
   'No,' she answered, 'I never eat more than one thing. Unless you had a little caviare. I never mind caviare.'
   My heart sank a little. I knew I could not . . .

Complete the last sentence.

- Did he persuade her not to order caviare?
- What did he order for himself?

By now, the reader will be starting to share the apprehension with which the writer was facing the meal ahead of him. We know that the conventional western meal has a structure ('sea beasts' to 'land predators and flying creatures' to 'cheese and artful puddings'). So, we anticipate that the meal may consist of more than the sea beast — i.e. the salmon — which he has ordered for his guest.

But his guest claims that she never eats 'more than one thing.' Or does she? Continue reading.

Part 5

My heart sank a little. I knew I could not afford caviare, but I could not very well tell her that. I told the waiter by all means to bring caviare. For myself I chose the cheapest dish on the menu and that was a mutton chop.

'I think you're unwise to eat meat,' she said. 'I don't know how you can expect to work after eating heavy things like chops. I don't believe in overloading my stomach.'

Then came the question of drink.

'I never drink anything for luncheon,' she said.

'Neither do I,' I answered promptly.

'Except white wine,' she proceeded as though I had not spoken. 'These French white wines are so light. They're wonderful for the digestion.'

'What would you like?' I asked, hospitable still, but not exactly effusive.

She gave me a bright and amicable flash of her white teeth.

'My doctor won't let me drink anything but champagne.'

I fancy I turned . . .

Task 3

Complete the last sentence in Part 5.

- Did he order the champagne?
- What did he order for himself?
- Why does he refer once again to her teeth?

Complete the following table.

What the woman says	What she asks for	How he reacts
'I never eat anything for luncheon.'		Orders it
		'My heart sank a little.'
		'I fancy I turned a trifle pale.'

By now a pattern has been established. The body of the story follows the structure of a meal. Throughout the story, there is a contrast between what the woman claims and what she actually does. This contrast, combined with what we know of the way a meal is typically organized, leads the reader to anticipate the outcome and to share the story-teller's growing sense of anxiety over his ability to pay the bill.

Task 4

Continue the story and end it with the following sentence:

To-day she weighs twenty-one stone.

Note that at the end, the present tense is used, although the main narrative is in the past tense. In fact, the time structure of the story is:

Opening: recent past
Body: distant past (flashback)
Ending: present.

When you have finished your version of 'The Luncheon', compare it with what other members of the class have written. Discuss why you continued the story as you did.

Task 5

After your discussion, read the complete version of the original story on pages 111–113 which Maugham wrote.
- How do your versions compare?
- How did Maugham imply that the woman was a glutton?
- Why did he write the story in the first person?

Although Maugham obviously drew on his own experience of being an impecunious young writer, all fiction writing is imaginative, that is, the writer uses his or her imagination to create an imaginary world. This world may seem very real to the reader, but it is still a product of the writer's imagination.

In some ways, when developing your skill as a short story writer, it is best not to base stories on your own life, but to write about things that you have not directly experienced. By putting yourself into situations outside your own personal experience, you have to use your imagination to create events, characters and feelings. This is what creative writing involves.

If you want to have an audience for a short story you write, and you live outside the United Kingdom, you can submit it to the BBC World Service programme called 'Short Story'. They want stories which are original, unpublished and have a local flavour. When read aloud, the story should take just under 15 minutes, which is about 2,000 to 2,300 words. Write to:

Short Story
BBC World Service
Bush House
London
UK.

Good luck!

THE LUNCHEON

I caught sight of her at the play and in answer to her beckoning I went over during the interval and sat down beside her. It was long since I had last seen her and if someone had not mentioned her name I hardly think I would have recognised her. She addressed me brightly.

'Well, it's many years since we first met. How time does fly! We're none of us getting any younger. Do you remember the first time I saw you? You asked me to luncheon.'

Did I remember?

It was twenty years ago and I was living in Paris. I had a tiny apartment in the Latin Quarter overlooking a cemetery and I was earning barely enough money to keep body and soul together. She had read a book of mine and had written to me about it. I answered, thanking her, and presently I received from her another letter saying that she was passing through Paris and would like to have a chat with me; but her time was limited and the only free moment she had was on the following Thursday; she was spending the morning at the Luxembourg and would I give her a little luncheon at Foyot's afterwards? Foyot's is a restaurant at which the French senators eat and it was so far beyond my means that I had never even thought of going there. But I was flattered and I was too young to have learned to say no to a woman. (Few men, I may add, learn this until they are too old to make it of any consequence to a woman what they say.) I had eighty francs (gold francs) to last me the rest of the month and a modest luncheon should not cost more than fifteen. If I cut out coffee for the next two weeks I could manage well enough.

I answered that I would meet my friend — by correspondence — at Foyot's on Thursday at half-past twelve. She was not so young as I expected and in appearance imposing rather than attractive. She was in fact a woman of forty (a charming age, but not one that excites a sudden and devastating passion at first sight), and she gave me the impression of having more teeth, white and large and even, than were necessary for any practical purpose. She was talkative, but since she seemed inclined to talk about me I was prepared to be an attentive listener.

I was startled when the bill of fare was brought, for the prices were a great deal higher than I had anticipated. But she reassured me.

'I never eat anything for luncheon,' she said.

'Oh, don't say that!' I answered generously.

'I never eat more than one thing. I think people eat far too much nowadays. A little fish, perhaps. I wonder if they have any salmon.'

Well, it was early in the year for salmon and it was not on the bill of fare, but I asked the waiter if there was any. Yes, a beautiful salmon had just come in, it was the first they had had. I ordered it for my guest. The waiter asked her if she would have something while it was being cooked.

'No,' she answered, 'I never eat more than one thing. Unless you had a little caviare. I never mind caviare.'

My heart sank a little. I knew I could not afford caviare, but I could not very well tell her that. I told the waiter by all means to bring caviare. For myself I chose the cheapest dish on the menu and that was a mutton chop.

'I think you're unwise to eat meat,' she said. 'I don't know how you can expect to work after eating heavy things like chops. I don't believe in overloading my stomach.'

Then came the question of drink.

'I never drink anything for luncheon,' she said.

'Neither do I,' I answered promptly.

'Except white wine,' she proceeded as though I had not spoken.

'These French white wines are so light. They're wonderful for the digestion.'

'What would you like?' I asked, hospitable still, but not exactly effusive.

She gave me a bright and amicable flash of her white teeth.

'My doctor won't let me drink anything but champagne.'

I fancy I turned a trifle pale. I ordered half a bottle. I mentioned casually that my doctor had absolutely forbidden me to drink champagne.

'What are you going to drink, then?'

'Water.'

She ate the caviare and she ate the salmon. She talked gaily of art and literature and music. But I wondered what the bill would come to. When my mutton chop arrived she took me quite seriously to task.

'I see that you're in the habit of eating a heavy luncheon. I'm sure it's a mistake. Why don't you follow my example and just eat one thing? I'm sure you'd feel ever so much better for it.'

'I *am* only going to eat one thing,' I said, as the waiter came again with the bill of fare.

She waved him aside with an airy gesture.

'No, no, I never eat anything for luncheon. Just a bite, I never want more than that, and I eat that more as an excuse for conversation than anything else. I couldn't possibly eat anything more — unless they had some of those giant asparagus. I should be sorry to leave Paris without having some of them.'

My heart sank. I had seen them in the shops and I knew that they were horribly expensive. My mouth had often watered at the sight of them.

'Madame wants to know if you have any of those giant asparagus,' I asked the waiter.

I tried with all my might to will him to say no. A happy smile spread over his broad, priest-like face, and he assured me that they had some so large, so splendid, so tender, that it was a marvel.

'I'm not in the least hungry,' my guest sighed, 'but if you insist I don't mind having some asparagus.'

I ordered them.

'Aren't you going to have any?'

'No, I never eat asparagus.'

'I know there are people who don't like them. The fact is, you ruin your palate by all the meat you eat.'

We waited for the asparagus to be cooked. Panic seized me. It was not a question now how much money I should have left over for the rest of the month, but whether I had enough to pay the bill. It would be mortifying to find myself ten francs short and be obliged to borrow from my guest. I could not bring myself to do that. I knew exactly how much I had and if the bill came to more I made up my mind that I would put my hand in my pocket and with a dramatic cry start up and say it had been picked. Of course it would be awkward if she had not money enough either to pay the bill. Then the only thing would be to leave my watch and say I would come back and pay later.

The asparagus appeared. They were enormous, succulent and appetising. The smell of the melted butter tickled my nostrils as the nostrils of Jehovah were tickled by the burned offerings of the virtuous Semites. I watched the abandoned woman thrust them down her throat in large voluptuous mouthfuls and in my polite way I discoursed on the condition of the drama in the Balkans. At last she finished.

'Coffee?' I said.

'Yes, just an ice-cream and coffee,' she answered.

I was past caring now, so I ordered coffee for myself and an ice-cream and coffee for her.

'You know, there's one thing I thoroughly believe in,' she said, as she ate the ice-cream. 'One should always get up from a meal feeling one could eat a little more.'

'Are you still hungry?' I asked faintly.

'Oh, no, I'm not hungry; you see, I don't eat luncheon. I have a cup of coffee in the morning and then dinner, but I never eat more than one thing for luncheon. I was speaking for you.'

'Oh, I see!'

Then a terrible thing happened. While we were waiting for the coffee, the head waiter, with an ingratiating smile on his false face, came up to us bearing a large basket full of huge peaches. They had the blush of an innocent girl; they had the rich tone of an Italian landscape. But surely peaches were no in season then? Lord knew what they cost. I knew too — a little later, for my guest, going on with her conversation, absentmindedly took one.

'You see, you've filled your stomach with a lot of meat' — my one miserable little chop — 'and you can't eat any more. But I've just had a snack and I shall enjoy a peach.'

The bill came and when I paid it I found that I had only enough for a quite inadequate tip. Her eyes rested for an instant on the three francs I left for the waiter and I knew that she thought me mean. But when I walked out of the restaurant I had the whole month before me and not a penny in my pocket.

'Follow my example,' she said as we shook hands, 'and never eat more than one thing for luncheon.'

'I'll do better than that,' I retorted. 'I'll eat nothing for dinner to-night.'

'Humorist!' she cried gaily, jumping into a cab. 'You're quite a humorist!'

But I have had my revenge at last. I do not believe that I am a vindictive man, but when the immortal gods take a hand in the matter it is pardonable to observe the result with complacency. Today she weighs twenty-one stone.

TEACHER'S GUIDE

UNIT 1

2 Different types of writing
Task 1

Text	Type	Features
1	postcard	message and address in separate sections handwritten very informal, short message
2	standard letter (i.e. sent out to more than one person)	typewritten/word processed impersonal style, e.g. salutation 'Dear Volkswagen owner', 'it is considered necessary for your vehicle to . . .'
3	report	typewritten use of headings and sub-headings to indicate purpose and topics detailed summaries of activities, etc.
4	examination answers	handwritten on special paper (N.B. special instructions to candidates — 'Do not write in this margin.')
5	newspaper advertisement	typeset lay-out — for easy reference abbreviations to save space (and money)
6	invitation	symmetrical layout and style of type formal language — 3rd person details of venue and time, type of clothes to wear

UNIT 2

2 Narrating events
Task 1
The questions which are answered by the text are:
When?
How?
Where?
How long?

Text 1 is an itinerary or plan of a journey. It is similar to a timetable, the difference being that a timetable is a plan for any journey, whereas an itinerary is a plan for a particular journey completed on one occasion. Since a journey also goes from one place to another, an itinerary will include information about space and movement.

Task 5
I was once having to travel between two small towns in southern Turkey and I was given as guides by the local police a small party of men who were going with an empty string of mules to pick up some grapes and bring them back. Since the mules were empty, they were able to take my gear and give me a lift too. We bargained for a price. It wasn't very much.

So, we stopped in the evening, after an afternoon's walk, and I had taken some tins of stuffed egg plants and a big water bottle. And, of course, we sat down, and I said, 'Please share my meal.' And, of course, they shared it.

And then, later in the night about midnight — I was pretty tired by this time — we came to a place where there were camp fires and one or two caravans around. And they said, 'We're stopping for a meal,' and they said, 'You can sleep over there.' So, I went to sleep.

Task 6
and, since, so, then

Task 9
read, assumed, called, got out, looked

3 Making a point
Task 2
comment 'but part of the fun of a bus trip is the element of magical mystery tour:'

Task 4
simile 'But a big orange-and-blue lifeboat stood poised like an exotic fish or bird;'

UNIT 3

3   Using anecdotes to make a point

Task 2

These people, for whom in many respects I have a great regard, are slightly less respectful to their travellers and to the sanctity of the road. A friend of mine who spent some time in that country just after the First World War — and before it, too, for that matter — told me that once he was travelling along a road with a local guide, and they came to a pile of stones recently put there which was clearly a grave. Normally in these circumstances this means somebody who has been found dead on or near the road, so he asked his guide if he knew the story behind this grave. He began to laugh and said he would tell what happened.

He said that there was a shepherd pasturing his flocks around here and two men came along and one said to the other, 'I bet that fellow's got some money on him. Let's waylay him.'

They started firing at him, but he began firing back from behind that rock and they couldn't really get him, but then one of the men said to the other, 'You keep him covered and I'll sneak around through that low ground and get up behind him, behind that rock up there, and catch him in the back.'

And he said he did this and he shot him and they robbed him and they buried him there.

'So,' my friend said, 'you seem to know an awful lot about this.'

'Naturally,' said the storyteller, 'I was the man behind the rock.'

Task 3

The introduction	Once he was travelling along a road with a local guide . . . .
Development	He said that there was a shepherd pasturing his sheep . . . .
Punch-line	'Naturally,' said the man, 'I was the man behind the rock.'

UNIT 4

2   Using language persuasively

Task 4

(Sample answer)

Sincere, English, unattached male, 47 and 5ft 7 tall, young looking and not unattractive, no ties, own house and car. Reasonably financially secure. Considered humorous, warm hearted, understanding and generous. Many and varied interests. Wishes to meet intelligent, attractive female, between 30 and 40. Status unimportant, but child welcome. Should live within 15 mile radius of East Croydon. Wishes to meet her with view to friendship and marriage. Photograph appreciated. All letters answered. Discretion assured. Box 7811.

UNIT 5

3   Arguing and suggesting

Task 1

d reasons
a example
d thesis/problem
b suggested solution
c example
The correct order is c, a, d, b

Task 3

First . . ., second . . .

Task 4

'both large and small, public and private'
'less painful, more palatable'

UNIT 6

3   Writing to the editor

Task 2

Paragraph	Function
4/5	Providing further evidence against the decision
6	Making an alternative suggestion
3	Describing the current situation and predicting the outcome of the recent decision
2	Reporting on a recent decision
1	Informing the reader of the topic of the letter.

X is not A, *but* it is B, *so* C is a consequence.
Y happens. *This will mean that* Z will follow.
People *rightly* believe that Z is D, *even though* people take care to avoid D.

Task 3

Rhetorical questions

'Can one be sure that no commuter, delayed by traffic, will never risk dodging through rather than miss his train?'
'Surely even one human life is worth that?'

Task 4

Text 1

The people of Etchingham share the anxiety . . .
British Rail could install a full-skirted, four-bar barrier at Etchingham.
British Rail tell us that closed-circuit television could control it.
British Rail also tell us that this would be too expensive.

Text 2

'The risks . . . when automatic half barriers *are installed are not supported* by experience.'

'There are . . . and since the first types *were installed* . . . no child pedestrian *has been killed* or even *injured* by a train at an automatic crossing.'

'Final approval *is* only *given* by the Secretary of State . . .'

'The proposal to install automatic crossing equipment . . . *has been subjected* to this rigorous procedure.'

'Councillor Moore . . . when the up-side car park *is closed.*'

If these were rewritten in the active voice, it would personalize responsibility for the installation of the barriers, etc. This is not the writer's intention.

Task 5

Objective	Subjective
'The independent Oppenheim report . . .'	'The widespread belief . . .'
'In that year . . .'	'The real threat . . .'

UNIT 7

2   Establishing and developing a theme

Task 2
The first sentences from the ensuing paragraphs are:

Bruner
"Why then invoke the idea of a 'will to learn'?"

Orwell
'Yet England, together with the rest of the world, is changing.'

Task 3

General	Specific
The environment	A journey by air
Food	Education for leisure and
Travel	unemployment
Success	Traditional arts and crafts in my
Pets	country
Problems	The environmental effects of acid rain
Computers	Famine, hunger and the provision of
Friendship	international relief
	The problems of being a stranger in a
	foreign country
	My favourite sport or game
	Changing patterns of child rearing in
	modern society
	A description of your town for visitors
	Overcoming examination nerves

3   Organizing ideas

Task 3

Example 1
New paragraph: 'The orderly came back in a few minutes . . .'
(further development of an action begun in the preceding paragraph)

Example 2
New paragraph: 'Parallel to geographical variation, we find social variation . . .'
(further development of an idea)

Example 3
New paragraph: 'Fire they made by . . .'
(new topic)

Example 4
New paragraph: 'A friendly approach to the dealer is probably best . . .'

Example 5
'But this raises the issue of competence, to which we must turn next.'
(Forward pointing reference)

Task 5
Example 1 Summing up (From *Toward a Theory of Instruction*)
Example 2 Looking to the future/Recommending (This is an extract from an editorial in *The Times*. It is not given elsewhere in the unit.)
Example 3 Summing up (*Language Change: Progress or Decay?*)
Example 4 Finishing the narrative (*News from Tartary*)

UNIT 8

2   Observing and noting

Task 9
'hanging bandoleer-style'
'old woman hobbling'
'a donkey cart . . . delivering sacks of laundry'
'workmen carrying bureaus, mirrors . . .'
'plumbers tearing up the side walk'
'housemaids . . . stopping to finger the furred rabbits'
'platforms holding two or three garbage cans'
'a pair of boys transporting a funeral wreath'
'guides talking into microphones'

noun phrases in which prepositional post modifiers are used
'a party of Swiss or German tourists'
'a party with cameras and other equipment'
'a party in their cleated shoes'
'sacks of laundry'
'artists from the Pensione Annalena'
'housemaids with shopping baskets'
'a funeral wreath in the shape of'
'big tourist buses . . . with guides'
'trucks of crated lettuces'
'trucks of live chickens'
'trucks of olive oil'
'a telegraph boy on a bicycle'
'a tripe vendor with a glassed-in cart'
'a man on a motorcycle with an overstuffed armchair'
'horse-drawn fiacres from the Pitti Palace'

UNIT 11

2 From brief to draft

Task 1

a 6, b 2, c 5, d 4, e 1, f 3

Task 7

1: a b (c) d e f g
2: a b (c) d e f g
3: b c g
4: a b c e f g

3 Making recommendations

Task 3

Summary B is more informative and helpful. It actually says what the students' problems are and what the report recommends. Summary A merely refers back to the body of the report.

Further reading

Peter Little (1977) *Communication in Business*, London: Longman.

Gordon A. Lord *It's My business to Know: Studies in Communication*

Sue Smithson (1984) *Business Communication Today*, Cambridge: ICSA Publishing.

Christopher Turk and John Kirkman (1982) *Effective Writing*, London: E. and F. Spoon

The idea of a 'pyramid of information' is taken from Turk and Kirkman.